MW00998127

BOWIE

THE ILLUSTRATED STORY | PAT GILBERT

chartwell
books

Inspiring | Educating | Creating | Entertaining

Brimming with creative inspiration, how-to projects, and useful information to enrich your everyday life, quarto.com is a favorite destination for those pursuing their interests and passions.

This edition published in 2020 by Crestline,
an imprint of The Quarto Group
142 West 36th Street, 4th Floor
New York, NY 10018 USA
T (212) 779-4972 F (212) 779-6058
www.Quarto.com

First published in 2017 by Voyageur Press, an imprint of The Quarto Group,
100 Cummings Center, Suite 265-D, Beverly, MA 01915, USA.

Chartwell titles are also available at discount for retail, wholesale, promotional, and bulk purchase. For details, contact the Special Sales Manager by email at specialsales@quarto.com or by mail at The Quarto Group, Attn: Special Sales Manager, 100 Cummings Center, Suite 265-D, Beverly, MA 01915, USA.

10 9 8 7 6 5 4 3 2 1

ISBN: 978-0-7858-3849-4

Acquiring editor: Dennis Pernu
Project manager: Jordan Wiklund
Art director: Cindy Samargia Laun
Cover illustration: Clémence Rolland
Cover design: Laura Drew
Interior design and layout: Brad Norr

Printed in China

Title pages: A young Bowie in London, 1966.
Copyright page: Performing "Rebel Rebel" on the Dutch TV show *TopPop*, Hilversum, the Netherlands, February 1974.
Table of contents: Onstage at Madison Square Garden, New York City, on the *Serious Moonlight* tour, July 27, 1983.

Contents

Introduction

When David Bowie passed away on January 10, 2016, two days after his sixty-ninth birthday, the outpouring of emotion was unusually intense. Something about Bowie's loss seemed uncommonly personal and deeply moving. It felt inconceivable that an artist with such limitless imagination and ceaseless drive could leave the world without any warning, having just released the brilliant, genre-defying *Blackstar*, his twenty-fifth studio album.

For fifty years, Bowie had been a byword for *cool*. Back in the early 1970s, he'd introduced the idea of adding theater to rock music when he assumed the character of the flame-haired, glam-rock messiah Ziggy Stardust. Thereafter came a series of iconic personas, each signaling an evolution in the form his music took. Aladdin Sane, with his razored-off eyebrows, distinctive lightning flash, and fluid sexuality, heralded a move into avant-garde art-rock. The zoot-suited "Gouster" image fanfared his dramatic left turn into contemporary American soul music. Then came the pale, alien-looking Thin White Duke, mixing soul, rock, esoterica, and electronica; the nameless, dressed-down hipster of his experimental Berlin Trilogy years; the Pierrot-costumed dandy of the New Romantic era; and the dashing men's fashion icon of the 1980s and beyond.

Each of these amazing transformations, which this illustrated history profiles, was propelled by a new philosophy, interest, location, or idea, usually coupled with the arrival of a different key musical collaborator, whether it was glam guitar god Mick Ronson, soul man Carlos Alomar, sonic visionary Brian Eno, punk avatar Iggy Pop, disco king Nile Rodgers, or multi-instrumentalist Reeves Gabrels.

But one thing remained constant: something in Bowie's music spoke directly, and intimately, to those who heard it. No one familiar with his catalog will ever forget the haunting image of the tragic astronaut Major Tom in his first hit, "Space Oddity," the "girl with the mousey hair" in "Life on Mars?," the lovers kissing by the Berlin Wall in "Heroes," or the Asian siren who sensuously whispers, "Shhh . . . shut your mouth" in

"China Girl." Nor will they ever forget the timeless, bewitching melodies of songs such as "Starman," "Golden Years," "Ashes to Ashes," "Loving the Alien," or "Little Wonder."

But while Bowie's extraordinary body of recorded work arguably remains unrivaled in music—as does his influence on street fashion—his work went way beyond the rock and pop world. From his teenage years, he was fascinated by film and theater, and in the 1970s and 1980s he enjoyed a parallel career as an actor, giving classic performances as John Merrick in the Broadway staging of *The Elephant Man* in 1980 and as the conflicted British army officer in 1983's *Merry Christmas Mr. Lawrence*. It was his starring role as the visiting alien in the 1975 cult movie *The Man Who Fell to Earth* that was his big-screen triumph, his character Thomas Newton blending with his own mid-'70s persona to create the otherworldly, drug-addicted Thin White Duke.

After Bowie's commercial peak in the mid-1980s with *Let's Dance* and *Tonight* and the hugely lucrative world tours that followed, his boundless imagination and artistic restlessness never waned, and lesser-selling later albums such as *1. Outside*, *Earthling*, and *Reality* demonstrated that he'd lost none of his gift for peerless artistry that had informed his 1970s and 1980s canon. His last two albums, *The Next Day* and *Blackstar*, suggested that he still had so much more to give the world had his life not been cut short by cancer. But then, as his friend and producer Tony Visconti points out, even Bowie's death was turned into a powerful artistic statement: the video for the *Blackstar* single "Lazarus" showed him writhing on a hospital bed, blindfolded, mouthing the chilling lyric, "Look up here, I'm in heaven."

Bowie was a one-off, a pioneer, a messenger, a starman, a charming English gentleman, and a genius. But for all his ever-changing looks, extraordinary musical innovations, and effortless personification of cool, he was also the suburban London boy next door who, as the story in this book shows, transformed himself by sheer willpower into an exotic, outlandish creature with a healthy and enthusiastic disregard for straight society's hang-ups and norms. Perhaps Bowie's death hit us so hard because, somewhere deep down in our souls, we know he was actually just one of us.

But, of course, he wasn't. He was David Bowie.

Pat Gilbert
London, February 2017

(opposite)
Angie, Zowie, and David at a press conference at the Amstel Hotel in Amsterdam, February 7, 1974.

1 9 4 7 – 1 9 6 7

London Boy

(opposite)
Performing on television for the first time as David Bowie, at a taping of *Ready Steady Go!*, March 4, 1966.

I t's perhaps fitting that David Bowie, an artist who combined music, image, theater, and myth with such boldness and originality, should have had a touch of the exotic in his background. At twenty-one years old, his father Haywood Jones, known as "John," inherited a sizeable sum of money, which he invested in—of all the options available in 1930s Depression-era Britain—a nightclub revue featuring his first wife, Hilda. Clearly the young Jones had a liking for music and colorful characters, for when that venture failed, he ploughed the £1,000 he had left into a glitzy piano bar in London's West End. But by the time World War II arrived in 1939, he'd lost all his money and taken a clerical job at Dr. Barnardo's, a famous charity that provided homes for abandoned and abused children.

Bowie's father left his job to fight in the war but returned to Dr. Barnardo's in 1945. Soon afterward, he met a waitress named Peggy Burns while on business in Royal Tunbridge Wells in Kent. Peggy already had a son, Terry, born in 1937, and a wartime daughter, Myra, who'd been given up for adoption. While the couple waited for John's divorce from Hilda to be finalized, they settled at 40 Stansfield Road, a Victorian house in inner-city Brixton that John had bought cheaply at the end of the war for £500. It was there that Peggy gave birth to a son, David Robert Jones, on January 8, 1947. Fair haired and nice looking, he would be the last addition to the family.

Terry Burns came to live with the family, but his presence caused friction with Bowie's father, by nature a reserved and taciturn character. John had fathered a daughter, Annette, in a prewar affair,

David Robert Jones in the mid-1950s, around seven years old.

and she too stayed at the house for a time. Stansfield Road was therefore a place of secrets and veiled tensions. But the overwhelming tone of Bowie's early home life—and the thing that also seemed to drive him to escape into the outlandish, colorful world of rock 'n' roll—would be something far more commonplace: the claustrophobia of drab, suburban normality.

Bowie was six when the family uprooted to Bromley, a small town on the edge of South London that by the 1950s had long been swallowed up by the ever-expanding metropolis. The Joneses eventually settled in a small terraced house in Plaistow Grove, just behind the Sundridge Park railway station. The area was characterized by its wide, leafy avenues and solid, middle-class homes, a stark contrast from the hubbub and poverty of war-damaged Brixton. Terry remained at Stansfield Road, ostensibly because of his job nearby, but also because the mental instability that characterized his adult years—and heavily shaded his younger half-brother's best work in the 1970s—was already making life for those around him difficult. But even without Terry, the mood at Plaistow Grove was subdued and oppressive.

Visiting the house in the mid-1960s, singer Dana Gillespie noted how joyless the house felt; John's history as a frivolous young nightclub impresario was long hidden behind the serious-minded front of a respected charity worker. "I went down to this little house, where everything was neatly laid out," recalled Gillespie, whose own parents enjoyed an affluent, bohemian lifestyle in West London. "There was plastic lino, which I hadn't seen before, and the sofa had one of those things to catch the Brylcreem. It was a place totally without humour or deep conversation."

Bowie admitted in later life to finding his mother, Peggy, emotionally distant and being unable to make conversation with his father, whom he nevertheless loved. There were also unspoken worries that Terry's illness, which ran through the Burns family line, might one day also claim Peggy or David. Plaistow Grove's strained atmosphere spurred the singer to greedily consume whatever entertainment was available, even if he had to create it himself. By the age of eleven, in 1958, he was already the proud owner of a ukulele and tea-chest bass, two key ingredients for making "skiffle," a homegrown hybrid of blues and country music popularized by Lonnie Donegan's hit cover of "Rock Island Line" in 1956. He also possessed a bag of records that his father brought home from work, the most thrilling of which was Little Richard's "Tutti Frutti," whose camp squeals and wild energy filled the house with what he described as "colour and outrageous defiance." Bowie was convinced at that moment that he'd "heard God."

The first hint that Bowie, who delighted in the fact that he shared a birthday with Elvis Presley, wanted to be a star himself came in August 1958. That month he entertained his fellow Boy Scouts around a camp campfire on the Isle of Wight, singing the Everly Brothers' "All I Have to Do Is Dream" and "Tom Hark" by Elias and His Zig

Zag Jive Flutes (both hits that summer). He was joined by his school friend George Underwood, who would be a close musical ally throughout his teenage years. A further sign that Bowie was eager to take an artistic path through life occurred around the same time, when he convinced his parents to let him enroll at Bromley Technical High School, even though his borderline exam results entitled him to attend the far more prestigious and academic Bromley Grammar School.

His choice of school turned out to be a crucial move: with its emphasis on creativity and craftsmanship, Bromley Tech boasted a first-class art department headed by forward-thinking teacher Owen Frampton, whose son Peter, later of the group Humble Pie and then a successful solo artist, joined the school in 1961. Bowie and his best mate Underwood enjoyed a schedule where whole days were sometimes spent in art classes. It was a progressive regime that, as Bowie later explained, "was an experiment to try to get us [pupils] involved in art at a younger age." Owen Frampton encouraged Bowie, Underwood, and Geoff MacCormack (another friend) to bring their instruments to school, where they'd harmonize rock 'n' roll hits in the echoey stone stairwell of the art block. Even at that tender age, to them the road ahead seemed straightforward. "We saw the glint of stardom and we wanted to go after it," Underwood recalled.

In 1959, Terry Burns had completed his compulsory three years' National Service and moved into Plaistow Grove. Together with a degree of disquiet, he also brought with him a collection of jazz records and beat literature, including Jack Kerouac's *On the Road*. These exotic totems helped fuel Bowie's growing fascination with all things American, including the newly appointed President Kennedy's haircut, which, to considerable amusement, Bowie requested at his local barber shop. He also developed a liking for baseball and American football—or at least the glamorous image of baseball players and NFL players—and wrote to the US Embassy declaring the fact. His enthusiasm was rewarded by an invitation to the embassy, where he and Underwood were each presented with an NFL helmet.

The visit made the local paper, an early instance of Bowie's knack for self-promotion and deep curiosity in subjects he'd quickly lose interest in. What remained constant was his obsession with music—everything from Charles Mingus and John Coltrane to novelty hits such as Anthony Newley's "Pop Goes the Weasel" and the caveman rock of the Hollywood Argyles' "Alley Oop." He was, increasingly, also fascinated with girls. It was the latter interest that led him to acquire a startling physical trait that in years to come would add immeasurably to his otherworldly allure.

The incident took place in the playground at Bromley Tech around Easter 1962, when Bowie and Underwood fell out over a

A key early influence, "Pop Goes the Weasel" by Anthony Newley.

girl they both fancied. Though each has given a different account of what happened, Underwood maintains that Bowie phoned him to say that his date with a girl named Carol was off—a fabrication, it transpired, to enable Bowie to snare her for himself. The ensuing row between the two boys boiled over into a fight, during which an irate Underwood threw a punch that connected with his friend's eyeball. The pupil in Bowie's left eye was permanently dilated as a result, giving his eye the appearance of having a different color—brown rather than blue.

Bowie was out of school for several weeks while he underwent treatment at London's Moorfields Eye Hospital, while a mortified Underwood tried to convince John and Peggy that he'd meant no real harm. "I was always looking at him thinking, oh God, I did that," Underwood told Paul Trynka, author of the acclaimed Bowie biography *David Bowie: Starman*. Later, Bowie would thank his friend for blessing him with "a kind of mystique," though in the immediate aftermath, they didn't talk for a while.

In the summer term, the guitar-playing Underwood joined the Kon-rads, a band that copied the beat and rock 'n' roll hits of the day. When the frosty relations between the two boys thawed, Underwood persuaded them to recruit Bowie, who by now had become proficient on a plastic alto saxophone his father had bought him two years earlier. It was wielding that instrument that Bowie made his first proper stage debut, at the Kon-rads' slot at a Bromley Tech school fete on June 16, 1962, honking along to a set of Shadows numbers.

Bowie's last year at school was dominated by dates with girls ("they loved him," a contemporary observed), trips to the record store in Bromley's Medhurst's department store, and rehearsals and gigs with the Kon-rads, who ironically booted Underwood out at the end of 1962 while keeping hold of his blond-haired, smartly dressed friend, now the proud owner of a proper brass tenor saxophone. Bowie—styling himself as "Davey J"—proved to be a huge hit with the group's female fans, who melted at his winning smile and young, pretty-boy looks. As Kon-rads singer Roger Ferris told *MOJO* magazine, "I was a better singer, but I had nowhere near David's personality and charisma on stage."

What many didn't recognize, however, was that Bowie's cool, easygoing manner masked what the singer would describe as "an unbearable shyness," which he disguised by throwing himself into roles and personas and which seemed to evaporate when he performed on stage. That autumn, the Kon-rads acquired a new drummer whose tenuous connection with fame deeply impressed their young saxophonist. "Dave Hadfield had apparently played with Cliff and the Shadows when they were called something else," Bowie informed the author in 2002. "He married one of our backing singers." Galvanized by the idea he might one day achieve similar fame, Bowie became ever more focused on becoming a star and began to take control of the group's direction. Intriguingly, the band caught the ear of Joe Meek, the visionary producer of "Telstar," but a demo session at his Holloway Road studio came to nothing. The group also auditioned for Decca with an

The Kon-rads play a school dance in Bromley, South London, in 1964.

original song called "I Never Dreamed," which Bowie may or may not have co-written (the jury's out on that one), but Decca wasn't impressed either. In late summer of 1963, the Kon-rads' swinging saxophonist quit.

Bowie's sudden departure baffled his bandmates, but in an interview years later, he revealed his reasoning was simple. As would happen again in the mid-1970s, he'd discovered the attraction of soul music. "I wanted to play [Marvin Gaye's] 'Can I Get a Witness' and they didn't," he explained to writer Paul Du Noyer. There may have been other things on the sixteen-year-old's mind too: that summer, he'd left school with just one O-Level pass—in art—and now had to face the unthinkable and find himself a job. Asked by his career advisor at school what he wanted to do, Bowie had replied, in all seriousness, that he wanted to be "a sax player in a modern jazz quartet." The closest to that position the advisor could find was a job at a harp factory in Bromley. Thankfully, his art teacher Owen Frampton intervened and arranged for Bowie to start work as a runner at an advertising agency on Bond Street in Central London. The idea of succumbing to the nine-to-five slog filled Bowie with horror. "I didn't wanna go down to Bromley South station and take the train to Victoria and work in a bloody advertising office," he told *Q* magazine's David Quantick.

Marc Feld, soon to be known as Marc Bolan, photographed in London in October 1965

Though Bowie "loathed it," the job meant he could spend his lunch hour exploring the music shops in London's West End. These included the storied Dobell's jazz record store on Charing Cross Road, where he picked up a copy of Bob Dylan's first album. The record had a profound effect: for the next few months, he and George Underwood, sporting jeans and cotton work shirts, performed raunchy folk and blues numbers as the Hooker Brothers (or else David's Reds and Blues). The ecstatic reaction from local audiences suggested they could do worse than expand into a fully electrified R & B combo. An advert in the *Melody Maker* soon led them to team up with a West London–based group called the King Bees.

As the King Bees' new singer and self-appointed leader, Bowie had the idea to approach a famous British entrepreneur of the time, John Bloom, with a view to Bloom managing the group. The text of his letter, drafted with the help of his father, ran along the lines of "Brian Epstein's got the Beatles, you need us." Bloom was impressed by their cheek and passed the missive on to his friend Leslie Conn, an associate of the Beatles'

The King Bees, again featuring George Underwood (left), perform "Liza Jane" on *The Beat Room*, summer 1964

Bowie's first recorded appearance (as Davie Jones) was the Vocalion single "Liza Jane."

publisher Dick James. The group was invited to prove its mettle at Bloom's wedding anniversary party at a Soho nightclub, where pop singer Adam Faith and World War II icon Vera Lynn were booked to top the bill.

The appearance was a disaster. Bloom was appalled by the King Bees' raucous, Stones-y racket and pulled the plug, but Conn loved them and offered to become their manager. As Bowie was only seventeen, Conn visited Plaistow Grove to obtain David's parents' signatures on the group's contract. Bowie immediately quit his job and took to hanging out at Conn's offices on Denmark Street, London's own Tin Pan Alley of music publishers, booking agents, and management companies. It was there that he first encountered another Conn protégé, Mark Feld—soon to rebrand himself as Marc Bolan—whose career was at a similarly embryonic stage. Conn gave the pair the job of painting his office "a shitty green" color, beginning their infamous fifteen-year friendship and rivalry.

"Marc was very much the mod and I was sort of neo-beat-hippy," Bowie recalled to *MOJO* regarding their initial clash of youth cults. "He went, 'Oh, I'm going to be a singer and I'm gonna be so big you're not gonna believe it.' Oh right! Well, I'll probably write a musical for you one day then, 'cos I'm going to be the greatest writer ever. It was all this. Just whitewashing walls in our manager's office."

Conn's involvement quickly paid off; Davie Jones with the King Bees, as they were billed, signed with Vocalion for a single, "Liza Jane," a reworking by Bowie and Underwood of an old folk song. Released in June 1964, it was an underwhelming vinyl debut for the future superstar—and an early lesson in sharp management practices, since Leslie Conn's name mysteriously appeared on the record as the song's author. Decca pushed the single hard, but even two TV performances, on *Ready Steady Go!* and *The Beat Room*, where Bowie cut a dash in knee-high suede boots and a leather jerkin, couldn't shift any copies.

When it was obvious the single was a flop, Bowie dramatically informed his bandmates he was quitting for pastures new. They were stunned. Underwood was particularly ruffled by his best friend's capricious behavior—though, thanks to Conn's help, the King Bees' demise enabled Underwood to enjoy a short-lived solo career as a protégé of producer Mickie Most before finding his vocation in the world of art. Bowie, meanwhile, headed off into deepest Kent to try his luck with a band he considered better attuned to the craze for tough, horn-driven R & B and soul music that was gripping mod-era Britain. The outfit, another in Conn's stable, was called the Manish Boys. Bowie met them on their home turf in Kent, where they made it clear they "didn't want him" as they already had a singer. Conn argued that Bowie's experience as a recorded artist and veteran of the nation's biggest TV music shows was exactly the injection of star quality

they required. So, in July 1964, Bowie jumped into the Manish Boys' beat-up Bedford van and spent the next twelve months gigging around the UK.

On stage, Bowie relished performing camp routines and winning over rowdy crowds, while off stage he gained a reputation as an incorrigible ladies' man, determined to bed as many admiring fans as he could. Women found his boyish charm irresistible. Singer Dana Gillespie first encountered him around this time backstage at the Marquee Club in Soho. "I was brushing my hair and he took the brush and carried on brushing," she recalled to writer Peter Doggett. "He asked if he could stay at my home . . . I had a single bed so it was a tight squeeze. His hair was so long my parents thought he was a girl."

In November 1964, Bowie's hair—uncommonly lengthy, even for a rocker—was the catalyst for an invaluable piece of free publicity. After kidding a reporter on the prowl on Denmark Street that he was a member of the Society for the Prevention of Cruelty to Men with Long Hair, he ended up appearing with his group on the primetime BBC television show *Tonight*. "We're all fairly tolerant," he deadpanned, "but for the last two years we've had comments like 'Darlin' and 'Can I carry your handbag?' thrown at us. It has to stop!"

The reality was far worse. Bowie, disposed to wearing his hair in girlish pigtails tied up with pink ribbons, had been punched in the street several times for his provocative looks. He didn't seem to care. The TV appearance brought him national attention, and the band was booked onto a package tour in December 1964 headlined by the Kinks and Marianne Faithfull. The momentum continued into January 1965, when Conn teamed them with the Who's producer Shel Talmy to cut a cover of soul singer Bobby Bland's "I Pity the Fool" and a zippy Bowie original, "Take My Tip." Future

Led Zeppelin star Jimmy Page, back then a session guitarist, appeared on the tracks but coolly informed the group that the record "wasn't a hit." He was proved correct, and after the single failed to make an impression, Bowie replayed his end game with the Kon-rads and King Bees and suddenly quit without ceremony. The last the Manish Boys saw of its hirsute singer was after a gig in Bletchley on April 24, when Bowie disappeared into the night with a female groupie.

Conn understood Bowie's frustration with the single's failure, but he also needed to keep him working. Outwardly, the singer appeared assured of his future stardom, but inevitably there were occasional flashes of self-doubt. "I might have moments of, God, I don't think anything is ever going to happen for me," he later admitted. "But I would soon bounce back." The bustling La Gioconda café on Denmark was the perfect spot to meet other musicians planning their next moves. While sipping a coffee, Bowie was noticed by members of the Lower Third, a singer-less group from Margate in Kent, who mistook him, as many did at the time, for the Yardbirds' Keith Relf. Discovering he wasn't Relf, but an experienced vocalist nonetheless, they invited him to an audition at the nearby La Discotheque on Wardour Street, a dingy club that had recently made the newspapers when its doorman was shot for refusing entry to a local Soho gangster.

The Lower Third's contract to appear at the Marquee in London, for a fee of £20 per night.

Bowie turned up with his friend Steve Marriott from the Small Faces in tow for moral support and impressed the band enough for them to agree to be his new backing outfit. In June, Davy Jones and the Lower Third set out on a string of dates in the Midlands and the South, but by this time, Conn had tired of life in band management and quit the business, annulling his contract with the singer. Enter another habitué of La Gioconda, Ralph Horton, a former road manager for the Moody Blues. Horton was a fascinating character, not least because he was a player on the Soho gay scene which Bowie had become a curious spectator of and sometime participant in. Even back in the Kon-rads days, Bowie had declared he was bisexual, with little

The Lower Third onstage at the Marquee in 1965.

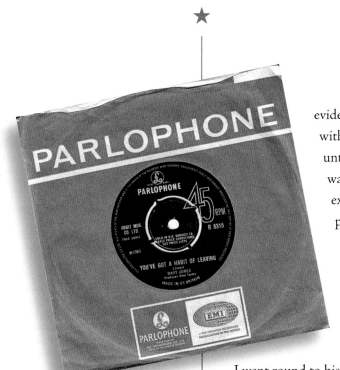

The Parlophone Records single of "You've Got a Habit of Leaving," credited to Davy Jones.

evidence to back up his claim. But with the Soho mod scene overlapping with underground gay culture—homosexuality was illegal in the UK until 1967—the taboo surrounding same-sex relationships was giving way to a thirst for experimentation. As the Who's Pete Townshend explained, "We thought David Bowie was gay. We thought all cool people were gay."

Horton began touting around his new charge, sensing he needed a more established manager to look after the business side of things. "I was managing the Yardbirds and received a phone call from someone I didn't know who introduced himself as Ralph Horton," Simon Napier-Bell recalled to the author. "He said he had an artist he was managing that he was sure I'd be interested in. I went round to his basement flat near Victoria station, down a few steps, a bit dingy. In the corner was a young man. Ralph introduced him as David and said in due course he'd be the biggest star in the world. If I would agree to co-manage him with Ralph I could not only have half the profits, I could also have sex with him. I turned and left. I never felt I'd turned down David Bowie because at that time Bowie didn't yet exist."

Bowie's metamorphosis into an increasingly exotic mod peacock—sharp suit, sculpted hair, Italian loafers—was accompanied by a new stage name, assumed in September 1965, a few weeks after Davy Jones and the Lower Third's first single, the Who-inspired "You've Got a Habit of Leaving," sunk without trace. The name change was motivated by a phone call Ralph Horton had made to his friend, Manfred Mann's manager, Ken Pitt, asking if he would help manage the singer. Pitt told Horton he was too busy at present, but did suggest Bowie should change his name; Pitt had read that a British actor named Davy Jones had just signed up to star in an American TV series about a fictional Beatles-style group called the Monkees.

David had been drawn to the name "Bowie" ever since seeing the 1960 film *The Alamo*, in which Davy Crockett (played by John Wayne) and Jim Bowie (Richard Widmark) stage a heroic defense of the titular fort. Jim Bowie had also given his name to the Bowie knife, the basis for the US Army's survival knife, further enhancing the name's dangerous magnetism. "It is the medium for a conglomerate of statements and illusions," Bowie floridly explained at the time. The first show with his new moniker was on September 21 at the 100 Club on London's Oxford Street, and though he would legally remain David Jones for the rest of his life, the stage name stuck.

Horton felt that Bowie would benefit from a different sound and introduced him to Tony Hatch, Pye Records' in-house producer/writer, whose own successes as a songwriter included the Searchers' "Sugar and Spice" and Petula Clark's "Downtown." The result was one of Bowie's finest pre-fame singles, "Can't Help Thinking About Me";

(opposite)
Bowie works on lyrics for his first album outside a café on Clapham Common, London, in 1966.

Davy Jones, as he was still calling himself, plays a Framus twelve-string acoustic, 1965.

Bowie and his latest group, the Buzz, at his old stomping ground, the Marquee, in April 1966.

the crooned verses and rowdy choruses showcased his characterful baritone, and the narcissistic, mod-minded title concealed a poignant account of his uncomfortable life at Plaistow Grove. Positive notices in the press failed to propel the single onto the chart, as did a launch party at Victoria Tavern near Hyde Park, attended by John Lennon's father, Freddie, then enjoying a brief rapprochement with his son. Though the party went with a swing, with Bowie applying his boundless charm to the music biz types and journalists in attendance, behind the scenes, his group was nearing mutiny.

If the Lower Third's credit on the single wasn't sufficiently demeaning—"David Bowie" appeared in large type, "With The Lower Third" in small type—then Horton's condescending attitude toward it underlined its place in the hierarchy. A loan from a London businessman, with vague terms that didn't require any repayment unless Bowie earned over £100 a month, had enabled the manager to indulge his enthusiasm for high living. Wild parties raged at his Warwick Square bachelor pad, and he bought a flashy Mk 10 Jaguar car. Little, if any, of this new wealth trickled down to the Lower Third. On a trip to Paris, Horton had whisked Bowie back to London in the Jag, leaving the

group to trundle home in their converted ambulance. Worse, in the last week of January, Horton refused to pay the group, claiming that their money had been swallowed up by expenses. A standoff took place before at show at Bromley's Bromel Club, and the Lower Third walked.

Bowie's reaction was typically airy and pragmatic: he simply advertised for replacement musicians in *Melody Maker*, consigning another backing group to the dustbin of history. The successful applicants, collectively christened the Buzz, promoted the Lower Third's single before backing Bowie on a second Pye release in April 1966, "Do Anything You Say," effectively David Bowie's first solo record since the Buzz was uncredited on the label. "Do Anything You Say" had none of its predecessor's élan, and it flopped. But it did coincide with Horton's friend Ken Pitt finally taking an interest in the singer.

The fateful meeting occurred at a Radio London–sponsored showcase at the Marquee Club, billed as the "Bowie Showboat." Pitt was deeply impressed with Bowie's performance, which ended with either a stirring version of "You'll Never Walk Alone" from the musical *Carousel* or else possibly Anthony Newley's "What Kind of Fool Am I?" (accounts differ), with Bowie dramatically illuminated in a spotlight. "Standing at the back of the Marquee, I realised straight away David was somebody very different," Pitt told journalist Chris Welch. "I'd never seen an artist like him. When the show was over and the people were leaving, David walked up to me and I was delighted to find he had an amazing sense of humour."

Unlike Horton, Pitt—a D-Day veteran—was an industry heavyweight who had worked in PR and promotion since the mid-1950s and was referred to by Frank Sinatra as "my man in London." His clients had included everyone from Liberace to Bob Dylan, and in recent years, he had steered Manfred Mann into the charts with "Do Wah Diddy Diddy." Pitt agreed to help manage Bowie, though it quickly became apparent that his and Horton's business affairs were in a parlous state. "The morning after our first meeting I had lots of bills arriving on my desk," Pitt explained to Welch. "They included one from Pye Records. It seems Ralph had purchased a large number of David's records and never paid for them. I also discovered they'd never paid their electricity bill so it was always being cut off. Not that there was much money coming in, but all the bills were paid."

In August, Bowie released another Tony Hatch–produced single, the funky swinging '60s wig-out "I Dig Everything," promoted with a nationwide tour. The song added to Bowie's growing pile of failures, so to bring in some much-needed cash, Pitt extended the band's concert schedule right through until December, when the singer declared he no longer wanted to play live and the Buzz quietly disbanded. By then,

The "I Dig Everything" single, released just before Bowie's twentieth birthday.

Released as a single in April 1967, "The Laughing Gnome" gave listeners an early taste of the sessions for Bowie's self-titled debut.

Bowie's first album—the one he'd later try to forget—David Bowie, released on June 1, 1966.

it had become clear why Bowie was ready to shed another skin: there had been a radical change in the style of songs he wanted to write and perform. Earlier in the year, Pye had passed on the opportunity to release a Bowie song called "The London Boys," a semi-spoken, semi-autobiographical tale of a seventeen-year-old leaving home for the pill-popping demimonde of Soho's back streets. In terms of lyrical depth, it was a huge leap forward for Bowie, and Pitt encouraged the singer to write more story-songs. A tape of "The London Boys" plus the equally theatrical but far stranger "Rubber Band" and "Please Mr. Gravedigger" convinced Decca's experimental offshoot Deram that Bowie, due to celebrate his twentieth birthday in January 1967, was finally coming of age as a songwriter.

By the time "Rubber Band" and "The London Boys" were bundled as a single in December 1966—which tanked—sessions for Bowie's self-titled debut album were already underway at Decca's studio in Hampstead, North London, overseen by producer Mike Vernon and engineer Gus Dudgeon. The influence of the Beach Boys' *Pet Sounds* permeated the new material, which forsook R & B in favor of complex baroque pop songs featuring quirky time signatures and woodwind, brass, and strings. The orchestrations were scored by Bowie along with the Buzz's bassist Dek Fearnley—neither of whom had previous experience producing charts for professional players.

An early taste of the sessions, "The Laughing Gnome," appeared as a single in April 1967 and has ever since been seized upon as evidence that Bowie had lost his marbles—though one wonders if this comedy record about "a little old man, in scarlet and grey" wasn't meant entirely as a joke, chiming as it did with psychedelia's obsession with childhood memories, fairy-tale creatures, and drug-induced visions.

Bowie's debut album, released on June 1 and simply titled *David Bowie*, proved to be similarly out there. Its fourteen songs, half-sung in a mannered London accent, inhabited a *Chitty Chitty Bang Bang*–type world where music hall, fantasy, and pop music converged. Unlike "The Laughing Gnome," however,

there was little to smile at. "Uncle Arthur," "Little Bombardier," and "Come and Buy My Toys" were unsettling vignettes of a dark adult world viewed through child's eyes; there were also traces of the dystopian sci-fi themes of Bowie's later work, most strikingly in "We Are Hungry Men," a disconcerting tale of a future race ensuring its purity through abortions and infanticide. Confusingly, the album also included the straight pop of "Love You Till Tuesday," the obvious choice for a single that July.

In the summer of 1967, *David Bowie* had stiff competition, not least from the Beatles' *Sgt. Pepper's Lonely Hearts Club Band*, released the very same day. But while *Sgt. Pepper* became the biggest-selling rock album of the 1960s, Bowie's first long-player stalled outside the UK Top 100 and remained a footnote in history until he became a star in the early 1970s. But, typically, by the time it appeared, Bowie had already moved on. The single "Love You Till Tuesday," another chart miss, was to be his last release for almost two years. Next came an extraordinary period that, though it bore little musical fruit, would nourish Bowie's artist impulses for many years to come.

A short press bio issued around the time of Bowie's Deram debut.

1 9 6 8 – 1 9 7 0

All the Madmen

(opposite)
Bowie outside the imposing entrance to Haddon Hall in Beckenham, South London, where he lived from October 1970 until spring 1973.

In the spring of 1967, Bowie's career took an intriguing new turn when Ralph Horton quit the music industry for a job in the motor industry, leaving Ken Pitt as Bowie's sole manager. For the next three years, it would be the urbane, gentlemanly Pitt who would steer the singer's career and help unlock the boundless creativity whirling around inside him. During this period, Bowie would experiment with mime, acting, scriptwriting, and even Buddhism, interests that would divert him from his music career but prove crucial to germinating the singular collision of rock, theater, costume, and mysticism that propelled him to superstardom in the early 1970s.

When Pitt took over, not long before the Deram release of *David Bowie*, he thought it appropriate to travel to South London to meet Bowie's father and reassure

him that, despite his son's poor record sales, his future lay in the arts. "We met at the local station," Pitt told Chris Welch. "He was a nice man, although I don't think he really understood what David was trying to do. He was nervous about the idea of David being in show business." A few weeks later, both to spare his parents from the noise of his nocturnal music sessions and to make space for his half-brother, Terry, who'd recently returned to Plaistow Grove after a serious mental episode, Bowie took up Pitt's offer of a spare room in his flat on Manchester Street in Central London. Ever supportive, and perhaps also glad of

Somebody up there likes me:
Bowie in Paddington, London, in 1968.

some peace and quiet, his father helped
Bowie move his belongings in his tiny
Fiat 500.

Pitt had long recognized that
his twenty-year-old charge had an
uncommon and far-reaching talent that
needed nurturing and that, after nine
flop singles, the time was right to explore
new artistic avenues. His attempts to
further the singer's career sometimes went
unappreciated, however. "We were invited
to a party attended by people who could
give David broadcasts and TV work," Pitt
recalled in *MOJO*. "I was chatting them
up, which was obviously a big bore for
him. Then a producer said, 'Is that your
wonderful David Bowie?' I turned round and saw him with some bird sprawled all over
him. I thought they were going to copulate in front of the British music industry. I left
without him."

Ken Pitt, who took over as Bowie's manager in 1967 and produced his first two albums.

Bowie spent his free days—of which there were plenty in 1967, after *David Bowie*
had slipped out largely unnoticed—devouring his host's impressive library of books
and classical records. Holst's *The Planets* suite became a particular favorite, as did Oscar
Wilde's *The Picture of Dorian Gray* and Saint-Exupéry's *The Little Prince*, and a book on
Egon Schiele, the controversial German painter who committed incest with his sister and
died at twenty-eight. Pitt's interest in art rubbed off on Bowie, who began to read about
the subject ravenously. A curious synergy between the two men was already becoming
apparent, as evidenced around Easter of 1967 when Bowie became the first musician ever
to cover a Velvet Underground track, at a time when Lou Reed's legendary group was
virtually unknown in its native Manhattan, let alone in London.

At the end of 1966, around the time the Buzz split up, Pitt had flown to New
York on business and took the opportunity to drop in at Andy Warhol's Factory. He
was given a signed test pressing of the then-unreleased *The Velvet Underground &
Nico* album, which he brought back to London. "Not being [Ken's] particular cup of
tea, he gave it to me to see what I made of them," Bowie informed the author in 2002.
"Everything I both felt and didn't know about rock music was opened to me on one
unreleased disc . . . . This music was savagely indifferent to my feelings. It didn't care if
I liked it or not." His mind blown, a few weeks later the singer recruited a band called
the Riot Squad to record a cover version of "Waiting for the Man" and a new song of his

own, "Little Toy Soldier," which liberally borrowed from "Venus in Furs." Nothing came of the project, but it was an interesting indication of how Pitt's and Bowie's enthusiasms interacted to make the singer even hipper than he'd been before.

Following the *David Bowie* album, Pitt brokered a new publishing deal with Essex Music, leading to a final session that year that produced the wonderful "Let Me Sleep Beside You." For Decca, the timeless, conventional rocker was too little too late, and it rejected it as a single (though Bowie would later tell a BBC interviewer it was never released because "my mother thought the lyrics were dirty"). Bowie's music career was, for the time being, put on ice; instead, he enjoyed his first taste of another area of performance that he seemed born to try: acting.

Pitt had always encouraged Bowie's wider interests in the arts, and one of Bowie's earliest excursions outside music was a radio play called *The Champion Flower Grower.* Though this was rejected by the BBC, Pitt saw Bowie's future in TV and theater. "David already wanted to be an actor and was capable of so many different things," Pitt told Chris Welch. "He wanted to write musicals. It was all down to evolution, and David was evolving constantly, sometimes from day to day. It was difficult to keep up with his train of thought." Rather than regard Bowie's Deram album as a failure, Pitt saw it as a useful CV of his talents. He bought fifty copies and distributed them to contacts in film,

Lindsay Kemp, Bowie's dance teacher and mentor in the late '60s, photographed backstage during a run of his show *Flowers* at the Bush Theatre, London, in 1974.

TV, and theater. One of the recipients was the mime artist Lindsay Kemp, with whom Bowie enrolled for dance lessons at his studio in Covent Garden. Kemp was yet to find the celebrity his appearance at 1968's Edinburgh Festival would bring, but the talented mime artist was already making waves on London's fringe theater scene.

Bowie and Kemp hit it off instantly, bonding over their love for musicals, the circus, Expressionist art, and Berlin cabarets. Bowie waxed lyrical about his newfound interest in Buddhism, then fashionable in hippie London, while the dancer turned his new friend onto Jean Genet, Jean Cocteau, and performance art. "I taught him how to project, to enchant and how to hypnotise the public when you

With his then-girlfriend, Hermione Farthingale, in their performance group at Turquoise, London, 1968.

step on to a stage," said Kemp, ten years Bowie's senior, to writer Martin Aston in 2004. "David absorbed everything, like a sponge." The pair began collaborating on a play titled *Pierrot in Turquoise*, for which Bowie provided music and took the role of Cloud. (Turquoise, the Buddhist symbol for eternity, reflected Bowie's influence on the project.) The work premiered at Oxford on December 28, 1967, before enjoying a two-week run in London in March 1968. During this time, Bowie had an affair with the openly gay Kemp, which ended in tears when Kemp discovered Bowie was also sleeping with the beautiful Russian set designer Natasha Korniloff.

Adding to the emotional tangle, Bowie had earlier in the year fallen for Hermione Farthingale, a striking red-headed dancer with whom, on Kemp's recommendation, he created a minuet for a BBC television play based on Alexander Pushkin's *The Shot*. After *Pierrot in Turquoise* ended its run, Bowie moved out of Pitt's home and took the top flat of a house off Old Brompton Road to live with Farthingale. Bowie spent a quiet summer enjoying his girlfriend's company, UFO-spotting on Hampstead with various acid-head friends, listening to Jacques Brel records (he'd discovered him via Scott Walker's albums), and sporadically performing his own mime routines at venues including the Middle Earth club and Roundhouse. He also appeared—fleetingly—as an extra in the film *The Virgin Soldiers*, for which he was required to have a military-style short-back-and-sides haircut.

Bowie's first forays into theater and acting had been less than stellar, and it hadn't escaped his notice either that while he was pursuing a life outside pop music, many of his direct contemporaries—including the Who and the Kinks, both of whom also released debut singles in 1964—had become internationally famous. That autumn, he was stung when another of

Photographed at home around the time of his first screen role in *The Virgin Soldiers*.

his peers, Marc Bolan, broke into the Top 30, with his duo Tyrannosaurus Rex's single "One Inch Rock." Bolan's success was the most painful for Bowie. The peculiar yin and yang of the two suburban Londoners' relationship can be sensed from an incident from around that time, when Bowie invited Bolan and his girlfriend June to spend the day at Farthingale's parents' house in rural Edenbridge, Kent. Without Bowie's knowledge, Bolan brought along his percussionist Steve Took and photographer Ray Stevenson and took over the Farthingales' verdant country garden for a photo shoot. Bowie felt he'd been used and stayed inside the house, while Bolan and Took posed flamboyantly outside in the shrubbery. "They never even spoke to David or thanked Hermione for the use of her parents' garden," observed Tony Visconti, the Brooklyn-raised producer who oversaw Bolan's records, in an interview with Bolan biographer Mark Paytress. Bowie, understandably, didn't speak to Bolan for several months afterward.

Bowie wrote few, if any, songs of note in 1968, but that winter, a haunting new tune could be heard wafting down from his and Hermione's top-floor flat. Written after Bowie had seen Stanley Kubrick's film *2001: A Space Odyssey*, released that year, "Space Oddity" told the story of Major Tom, an astronaut who after blasting into the sky ends

Bowie gives a mime performance at the Middle Earth in London, May 19, 1968.

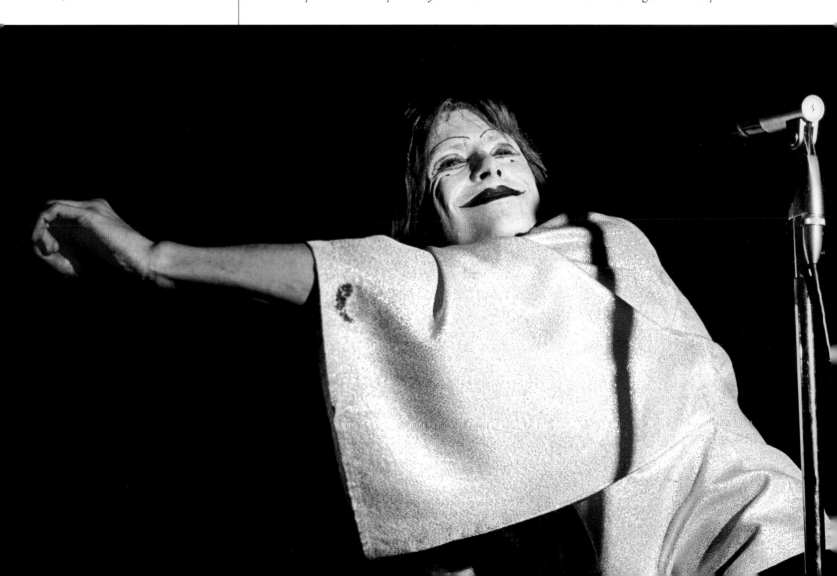

up drifting alone in space, never to return to Earth. Both endearingly childlike and devilishly clever, musically and lyrically, it eclipsed everything Bowie had previously written. At its heart were profound questions about the space race: What did it all amount to? What did winning it mean?

In January 1969, Ken Pitt began assembling material for a short demonstration film, *Love You Till Tuesday*, to promote Bowie's talent as a multifaceted, all-singing, all-dancing, all-miming artist. Several segments featured David, Hermione, and the Buzz's John "Hutch" Hutchinson performing new songs and a mime routine as "Feathers," while another saw Bowie, dressed in white tights and a codpiece, acting out a piece he'd devised called *The Mask*—a prescient comment on the price that fame exacts, ending with the protagonist's death on stage. Promo clips were also created for the two-year-old chart miss "Love You Till Tuesday" and unreleased "Let Me Sleep Beside You." Pitt asked the film's director, Malcolm

A promotional photograph taken during the period between Bowie's first and second self-titled albums.

Thomson, for another song to complete the show reel; he suggested "Space Oddity," which he'd heard the singer strumming. "David sat on the edge of my chaise longue and sang me 'Space Oddity,'" Pitt recalled to *MOJO* of the song's audition. "It was incredible." A sequence with Bowie dressed as a spaceman was duly shot to accompany an early demo version of the song.

Viewed today, the *Love You Till Tuesday* film is a fascinating period piece, oozing 1960s grooviness while rather gauchely marketing its twenty-two-year-old subject as an all-around entertainer. The month it was shot, Bowie appeared in a TV commercial for Lyons Maid's Luv ice cream, seemingly just the kind of job the film aimed to bag him. Bowie remembered it as "a happy time," but not long after *Love You Till Tuesday* was finished, Farthingale dropped the bombshell that she'd been offered a part in the movie version of the *Song of Norway* musical and was leaving for location shooting overseas. When she fell in love with an actor on set, it spelled the end of their relationship.

Bowie later admitted to being "devastated" by the breakup, so much so that he underwent a radical image change and had his hair permed. But he soon moved on. A few weeks later, while visiting an old friend in Beckenham, near his parents' home in Bromley, one of the neighbors heard him playing the guitar. She introduced herself

A still of Bowie performing "Space Oddity" in the half-hour promotional film *Love You Till Tuesday*, shot in 1969 but not released in full until 1984.

Bowie (left) with Hermione Farthingale (center) and John Hutchinson (right) in the dance/folk group Feathers, 1968.

as Mary Finnigan, a writer for the counterculture newspaper the *International Times*, and offered Bowie some cannabis oil. They began an affair and Bowie moved into her flat, which she shared with her two small children. The previous December, Bowie and Farthingale had staged two Arts Lab events in Central London featuring mime, poetry, Buddhist chants, and music, and now Bowie proposed to Finnigan that they revive the idea in suburban Beckenham. In May 1969, Finnigan booked the back room of the mock-Tudor pub, the Three Tuns, in the town center for a series of weekly Sunday evening gatherings. "Come for the fun of it and for instant identification with the vibrations," ran the publicity blurb, with Bowie declaring that the Arts Lab should "take over from the youth club concept as a social service." The hippie happening, where Bowie would perform on his twelve-string acoustic guitar, proved a winner and became a regular weekly gig. It did little to raise Bowie's profile outside South London, of course, but it did mean he was playing music again. Show reel in hand, meanwhile, Ken Pitt was busy trying to secure a new record deal on the strength of "Space Oddity." He found a useful ally in Calvin Lee, a colorful music industry character who wore a glittering circle on his forehead—as Bowie would in 1973. Through Lee's contacts at Mercury, Pitt was able to negotiate a contract with its UK partner Philips with a view to release "Space Oddity" to coincide with NASA's proposed moon landing in July 1969.

Tony Visconti, now a good friend of Bowie's, was tasked with recording the song. Dismissing it as a novelty record ("a cheap shot"), he passed the job on to Gus Dudgeon. Assembling a crack team of session men, including bassist Herbie Flowers and keyboard player Rick Wakeman, then still at music college, Dudgeon nailed the session, complete with Bowie's futuristic parts played on a new toy electronic instrument, the Stylophone. The single was released on July 11 and used during the BBC's coverage of the moon landing nine days later, which, like most of Britain, Bowie stayed up all night to watch. Just in case the launch ended in tragedy, BBC Radio wouldn't play the record until the Apollo 11 astronauts had safely returned to Earth, which slowed the single's ascent on the charts. In fact, it wouldn't be a hit until October, when it reached No. 5 in the UK. In the United States, jittery executives at Mercury demanded an edit that fudged Major Tom's unpleasant fate, then got cold feet and refused to promote the release.

While "Space Oddity" floated up the UK charts, Bowie's life changed immeasurably due to two dramatic events: first, the death of his father from pneumonia on August 5 and, second, his deepening relationship with Angie Barnett, the American girlfriend of Bowie's music industry champion Calvin Lee, with whom Bowie had enjoyed a brief liaison. He would later quip that he and Angie met "because we were both fucking the same bloke." Both Haywood Jones's passing and Barnett's arrival cast shadows over the free festival Bowie staged on Saturday, August 16, at Beckenham Recreation Ground, just a two-minute walk from the Three Tuns pub. Several thousand souls turned up to Bowie's answer to Woodstock—taking place in Upstate New York that same weekend—to watch performances by Bowie and folk artists the Strawbs, Keith Christmas, and Bridget St John, and soak up the hippie vibes.

Bowie gives a reading at Beckenham Arts Lab during the spring of 1969, a few months before the release of his era-defining "Space Oddity" single.

The original Phillips release of "Space Oddity," backed with "Wild Eyed Boy from Freecloud."

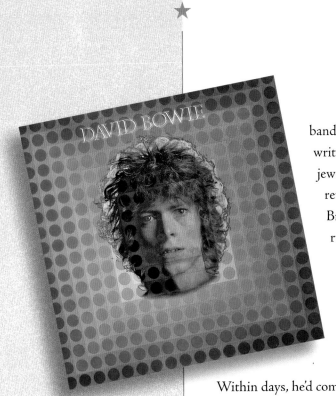

Bowie's second LP was initially released in the UK as *David Bowie* and in the US as *Man of Words/ Man of Music*, but has been known since 1972 by the title of its most famous song, "Space Oddity."

"In the middle of the little green was a beautiful pagoda like bandstand, where we all sat and played," recalled Bridget St. John to writer Lois Wilson in 2016. "Then surrounding it were stalls selling jewellery and ceramics. . . . there were Tarot readings, astrologers, the retail shop. Angie was making hamburgers in a wheelbarrow, the Brian Moore Puppet Theatre performed, there were lots of kids running around. It was a really beautiful day."

But Bowie's mood darkened as his own headlining appearance approached. His father's funeral had taken place just a few days before, and an Arts Lab associate remembers the singer being "detached. He wanted to go home." When Bowie spotted Mary Finnigan and Lee totaling up the day's takings, he blasted them as "materialistic wankers." The dark cloud quickly passed. Within days, he'd commemorated the event in a new song, "Memory of a Free Festival," in which he reminisced, "It was ragged and naïve / it was heaven." The song was among the last recorded for a new album he'd been working on at Trident Studios in Soho, with Visconti in charge. The producer recalled the music taking shape haphazardly; Bowie sat on a stool strumming his twelve-string while the musicians around him—essentially the same crew that cut "Space Oddity"—fleshed out the arrangements. One new recruit was Keith Christmas, one of Bowie's favorites from the Arts Lab and its attendant festival.

"David wasn't a guy that was particularly easy to know," Christmas told the author. "He was quite a guarded soul but also very engaging and easy to be around. I remember we worked in the studio pretty spontaneously. There were two seats and just three mics—one on David's guitar, one for his vocal, and one on my guitar. I hadn't heard the tracks at all. He played 'Letter to Hermione' first and tried some different things out. I did this run that we liked and became part of the song. We made it up as we went along."

None of the new songs quite topped the progressive, science-fiction magic of "Space Oddity," but the music had impressive depth and originality. The confessional "Letter to Hermione" and euphoric psychedelic rave-up of "Memories of a Free Festival" were evidence of Bowie's unusual melodic and harmonic approach, and the ambitious prog-folk opus "Cygnet Committee," with its embittered hippie messiah figure and cynicism about the counterculture, provided the first glimpse of the dystopian ideas more fully explored in the key Bowie records of the early 1970s. Strong echoes of Dylan reverberated around "Unwashed and Somewhat Slightly Dazed" and "God Knows I'm Good," but the overall flavor of the record—as good a musical summation of 1969 as any other, if a somewhat uneven affair—was all Bowie's own. The album was released in November 1969, confusingly with the same title in the UK as his 1967 Deram album, *David Bowie*, while in the States it was bestowed the appalling name *Man of Words/*

(opposite)
A promotional shot of Bowie and his trusty twelve-string, taken around the time of the release of his second album.

Man of Music. Not that it mattered, as it didn't sell in either territory. Visconti's fear that "Space Oddity" would mimic the fate of most novelty records was proved correct too, and Bowie wouldn't see the higher reaches of the charts again for another three years.

Following his father's death, Bowie and Angie Barnett had moved into Plaistow Grove to look after Peggy, but at the end of September, they took out a lease on their own home, a capacious ground-floor flat within a crumbling, converted Edwardian mansion in Beckenham, with the grand name Haddon Hall. Within the walls of this neo-Gothic palace, lit at night by candles and flames from its large open fireplace, Bowie would spend much of late 1969 and 1970 in semi-reclusion, fermenting the ideas that would shape his future work. Playing a major part in his development was the formidable Barnett, who increasingly exerted her influence over Bowie's career choices, much to the annoyance Ken Pitt. Loud, smart, and domineering, Barnett had arrived in London in 1967 to take a business course but soon found her way onto the music scene. Her bright mind and indifference to Bowie's promiscuity—she herself was bisexual and uninhibited—made her an attractive partner, and Bowie's feelings for his new girlfriend were encapsulated in one of the few new songs he wrote in the winter of 1969/1970, "The Prettiest Star," a nostalgic rock 'n' roll number recorded at Trident on January 8, 1970.

Now back on equal pegging with Marc Bolan thanks to "Space Oddity," Bowie agreed to Visconti's suggestion that Bolan play electric guitar on the track. The session was good humored—it was, after all, Bowie's twenty-third birthday—until Marc's girlfriend June screamed at the playback, "This song is crap! The best thing about it is Marc's guitar!" Bolan didn't demur and packed his guitar away, and the couple left without bidding goodbye. As far as Bowie was concerned, "The Prettiest Star" had already worked its magic, since at Christmas Barnett had agreed to marriage after he had serenaded her with the song over a telephone line, as she was abroad visiting family at the time. At Haddon Hall, the couple's nest building continued apace, the royalties for "Space Oddity" now flowing in, funding shopping sprees for expensive antiques, rugs, drapes, and furniture. One purchase was a seven-foot Regency bed, conveniently sleeping three or more. For the first time in his life, Bowie had money in the bank, and he enjoyed spending it. He took driving lessons, passed his test, and brought a car. Meanwhile, he continued to perform at the Arts Lab every Sunday evening, drawing crowds curious to see Beckenham's biggest star.

Bowie's casual approach to life was a hallmark of his early days—as were unexpected strokes of luck that would prove critical in advancing his career. The BBC approached him to headline a prestigious new *In Concert* radio program on February 5. The singer needed a band and recruited Visconti on bass and drummer John Cambridge from Junior's Eyes, who had backed him on an autumn promoting *David Bowie.* The job of guitarist was initially to be filled by Junior's Eyes' Tim Renwick, but Cambridge proposed instead they audition a musician he knew in Hull. So Cambridge headed 150 miles north to seek out the Rats' Mick Ronson, an extraordinary guitarist who was set to play a huge part in Bowie's story.

In early 1970, Ronson had all but retired from music and was making a steady living working for the local council marking out rugby pitches. Having made little money from the no-hope bands he'd played in, he was reluctant to re-enter the world of rock 'n' roll, but Cambridge persevered, luring him to the capital on February 3 to watch Bowie at the Marquee. After the show, Ronson returned to Haddon Hall, where a late-night jam convinced Bowie that "Ronno" was the missing ingredient they needed. The following day, the band frantically rehearsed for the radio show, tackling several tunes from Bowie's last album and a new song, "The Width of a Circle." Bowie also rehearsed a solo version of Jacques Brel's "Amsterdam."

The Hype—featuring Tony Visconti on bass—at the Roundhouse, London, in March 1970.

At the recording, Bowie warned the audience that he'd met his guitarist "Michael" only two days before, but the performance proved to be electrifying. With Ronson now on board, Bowie prepared for a gig at the Roundhouse two weeks later supporting ex–Jimi Hendrix Experience bassist Noel Redding's band Fat Mattress. Bowie decided would be his own group's inaugural show as the Hype, a name suggested by Ken Pitt after Bowie had told him, "This needs a strong element of hype," or something to that effect. The Roundhouse concert on February 22 has gone down in history as a potential candidate for glam rock's Big Bang. Tickled by the idea that the group should dress up as cartoon characters, Angie Barnett ventured into London to purchase suitable garments which she and Visconti's partner Liz Hartley then ran up into stage costumes. "David was Rainbow Man, dressed in Lurex, pirate boots and with diaphanous scarves pinned to his clothes," Visconti recalled to Mark Paytress. "I was Hype Man in a mock Superman costume with a white leotard, crocheted silver knickers and a big red cape." Meanwhile, Cambridge appeared as Pirate Man, and Ronson, his guitar turned up deafeningly loud, was a Chicago gangster. "I thought it would be interested if each of us adopted a persona," Bowie later recalled, "because it was all jeans at the time. But we got booed all the way through the show. People loathed what we were doing. It was great!"

The Hype's extravagant threads and heavy-metal thunder may have been two years ahead of their time, but there could be little excuse for the audience reportedly booing "Quicksand," one of the finest songs Bowie would ever write, granted its first airing that night with a full band arrangement. But the Roundhouse and other Hype shows in the following weeks did little to help the cause of "The Prettiest Star" single, which leaked out in March 1970 and whose failure—it sold only a few hundred copies—all but ended Bowie's faith in Ken Pitt to oversee his career. Pitt's suspicions that his managerial role was threatened were confirmed on March 20, when Bowie and Barnett married at Bromley Registry Office, having spent the previous night in a threesome with an actress following a show at the Three Tuns. Pitt only heard about the wedding secondhand and was deeply

A poster advertising Bowie's September 1970 performance at what would become a regular haunt, Friars in Aylesbury.

The UK and US editions of Bowie's third album, *The Man Who Sold the World*. For the British edition, Bowie was photographed wearing a dress by fashion designer Michael Fish; the American release features a cartoon image by Bowie's friend Michael J. Weller.

hurt. The sense that an era in Bowie's life was ending was underlined by the closure of the Arts Lab, which, Bowie felt, had lost its numinous qualities and was now simply an opportunity to see Bromley's famous one-hit wonder in person.

Bypassing Pitt, Angie badgered Philips directly for a £4,000 advance to fund the Hype's living expenses and some new recordings. The label coughed up, and the group began work in the tiny room under the staircase at Haddon Hall, now transformed into a makeshift rehearsal room/studio. The first fruits included a new arrangement of "Memory of a Free Festival," which was released in the United States as a follow-up to "Space Oddity." A radio recording in late March convinced Ronson that John Cambridge wasn't up to the job, and he was replaced by another drummer from the Hull music scene, Woody Woodmansey. After intensive rehearsals, sessions for what would become *The Man Who Sold the World* began at Trident in April, with Ronson driving the songs forward with his fluid, transformational guitar playing. Visconti would later gripe that Bowie, distracted by his infatuation with Barnett, had limited input into the backing tracks for the hard rockin' "She Shook Me Cold" and "Black Country Rock" or the prog-rock excursions within "The Width of a Circle."

But the end results were remarkable. *The Man Who Sold the World* was unquestionably Bowie's first classic album, a dark, psychologically complex work where science-fiction, theosophy, and empathy with society's outsiders collided, and a warm (if dysfunctional) human spirit prevailed. Bowie's interest in Buddhism and the occult permeated the disturbing visions of "The Width of a Circle," where the narrator seemingly has sex with Satan—or God, or himself—while the chilling "Saviour Machine" described a dictator who builds a computer that turns on the human populace. "The Supermen"—using a chord change "given" to the Bowie by Jimmy Page at the session for "I Pity the Fool" back in 1965—referenced Nietzsche's idea of the exiled super-race so beloved by the Nazis.

It was "All the Madmen" that was the most revealing song lyrically, though few outside Bowie's inner circle could have guessed its significance. In early 1969,

Bowie's half-brother, Terry Burns, had become a regular visitor to Haddon Hall at a time when his mental state was fast deteriorating. The first indication of his worsening schizophrenia had been an episode in 1967, when on a visit to Chislehurst Caves he saw Christ, then a vision of the ground opening up before him revealing the fires of hell burning down below. After sleeping roughly for a week, he turned up at Plaistow Grove, where Bowie was profoundly shaken by the sight of his deeply distressed sibling (it was soon after this that Bowie moved in with Ken Pitt). Burns was subsequently treated at Cane Hill psychiatric hospital, a grim former Victorian lunatic asylum a few miles away from Bromley. The references to the "cold and grey" Cane Hill in "All the Madmen" are clear, and Bowie's sympathy for his brother's illness, coupled with an awareness of his own possible proximity to madness, is deeply touching. Yet its inspiration remained hidden to outsiders, as did the origin of the line, "He struck the ground, a cavern appeared / And I smelt the burning pit of fear," in "The Width of a Circle."

The conclusion of *The Man Who Sold the World* sessions—with Bowie's vocal takes for the title track a disquieting meditation on being, identity, and death—coincided with Pitt's formal dismissal in May. The *coup de grâce* came from a litigation clerk named Tony Defries, whom Bowie appointed as his legal advisor on the advice of Olav Wyper at Philips. The showdown took place at Pitt's home on Manchester Street, where the manager agreed to step aside—if he was adequately compensated for the time and money he'd invested in his charge. Defries, the forthright son of a West London antiques dealer, assured Pitt that they could come to an arrangement. Defries's next move was to inform Bowie's publisher Essex Music that the singer would not be renewing his contract with them. (A lengthy legal battle ensued, eventually settled by Essex acquiring ownership of several Bowie songs.) Visconti, who retained close ties with Essex, was unimpressed with Bowie's new legal advisor and buried himself in other projects. Adding to the confusion, that summer Philips dismissed Wyper, one of Bowie's few fans at the label, leaving the tapes of *The Man Who Sold the World* in limbo. Ronson and Woodmansey signaled their unease with Bowie's floundering career by moving back to Hull; when they did return to London later that year, it was to record a single with their new band, Ronno. The producer was none other than Tony Visconti, no longer a lodger at Haddon Hall and busy working with Marc Bolan's T. Rex.

Typically relaxed, Bowie shrugged off the departure of his key musical allies and spent the summer of 1970 ensconced with Angie in their strange, suburban imaginarium—whose bedroom was likened by one visitor to "Dracula's living room"— where they hosted sex parties and held late-night discussions on philosophy, religion, and the occult. Occultist diviner Aleister Crowley's concept of enlightenment via sexual intercourse—so-called "Sexmagick"—was enthusiastically explored, though by day Bowie wasn't beyond more prosaic preoccupations such as fiddling around under

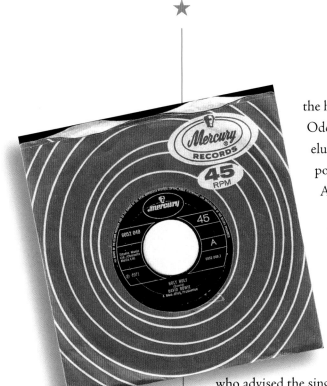

The first fruits of Bowie's new deal with Chrysalis: the "Holy Holy" single.

the hood of his old Riley sports car. A year after the release of "Space Oddity," it once again looked as if sustained success was destined to elude Bowie. Without an album to promote, or a band, he saw little point in playing live, and besides a handful of solo shows in July and August, he retreated from public view.

His inaction wouldn't last long. In October, Defries netted Bowie a publishing deal with Chrysalis, which came with an astonishingly generous advance of £5,000. Chrysalis's liberal terms reflected the enormous potential that one of the company's partners, Bob Grace, saw in the singer. Over the next few months, he encouraged Bowie to disregard himself as a budding pop star and instead view himself as one-man Brill Building, writing hit material for other artists. This was more than fine with Defries, who advised the singer to wait until his contract with Mercury expired the following June before he recorded another solo album. Grace also arranged access to Radio Luxembourg's demo studios in Mayfair, a welcome progression from the makeshift facility under the staircase at Haddon Hall. The first song recorded under Bowie's new contract was "Holy Holy," featuring Herbie Flowers on bass and, doing his old boss a favor in between his Ronno work, Mick Ronson on guitar.

Bowie and Grace's relationship fast evolved into a close friendship, permitting the publisher a unique insight into the singer's increasingly otherworldly existence. On several occasions, he accompanied Bowie and Angie—now pregnant—to outré night spots such as El Sombrero in Kensington, where they'd hang out with London's fashionable gay elite, including *Oliver!* composer Lionel Bart, the Who's manager Kit Lambert, and fashion designer Ossie Clark, as well as exotic young scenesters such as stylist Freddie Burretti and boy-about-town Mickey King. At this time, Grace believed that Bowie "was convinced he was bisexual," though others, such as his Beckenham Arts Lab partner Mary Finnigan, preferred to consider his bisexuality "opportunistic and contrived." Bowie, of course, reveled in the confusion his flirtation with gay society provoked and relished even more the strange looks he received for wearing the latest addition to his wardrobe—a velvet "man-dress" from the Mr. Fish boutique in Mayfair.

If Grace was struck by Bowie's flamboyant social circle and intriguing sexual ambiguity, he was even more impressed by Bowie's determination to develop as a songwriter. Previously, the singer had tended to write songs on the twelve-string guitar, but in the weeks leading up to Christmas 1970, he acquired a piano and installed it in Visconti's old room at Haddon Hall, overlooking the back garden. With the pregnant Angie attending his every need, he would sit for hours each day toying with unusual chord sequences and melodies. It was amid this period of suburban exile and periodic

dissipation that the first songs for *Hunky Dory* and *Ziggy Stardust*, his first truly great works, began to take shape. "I forced myself to be a good songwriter, and I became one," Bowie admitted to *MOJO* in 2002 of his determination to improve his craft. "I made a job of work, of getting good."

Yet Bowie's new life as a cross-dressing, stay-at-home songwriter was soon interrupted by the unlikely intervention of Mercury's offices in New York. In November, although still not available in the UK, *The Man Who Sold the World* album, with a cartoon cover by artist Michael J. Weller showing a cowboy and Cane Hill hospital, had crept out in the United States, selling a somewhat risible 1,300 copies or so. Bowie and Defries had already discussed the idea—or, at that time, possibly the fantasy—of breaking the singer in the United States before launching him in Britain, so when a call came from Mercury's publicity department suggesting a short US promo trip to boost the album's profile, Bowie jumped at the chance. The singer arrived in the country that had enchanted him since boyhood on Wednesday, January 27, 1971, only to be greeted by an hour's wait at Washington Dulles International Airport while customs officials

Bowie and his new American wife, Angie (born Mary Angela Barnett), at Haddon Hall in 1971.

(opposite)
Bowie performs at a party for deejay Rodney Bingenheimer in Los Angeles, January 1971.

tried to figure out why their London embassy had issued a visa to an unknown foreign musician with women's clothing and flowing long blond hair. Unusually, the ever-forceful Angie wasn't there to be in her husband's corner; five months pregnant, she'd opted to stay at home in London. Absent too was Defries, leaving Bowie to make his grand adventure alone.

The promotional tour, organized by Mercury's new PR agent Ron Oberman—a fervent Bowie apostle—moved on from the US capital to Philadelphia, New York, Detroit, Chicago, Milwaukee, and Houston before winding up in San Francisco and Los Angeles. In New York, Bowie was introduced to the eccentric musician-poet Moondog and was thrilled to watch his heroes the Velvet Underground perform at the Electric Circus, cornering its ice-cool frontman afterward to explain what a huge fan he was. Only later would he learn that he'd been talking to Doug Yule and not Lou Reed, who had left the group a few months before. For the West Coast leg of his trip, Bowie was shadowed by Rolling Stone writer John Mendelsohn, who was intrigued to discover that the obscure British "folk singer" he'd been dispatched to meet at San Francisco International Airport wore a dress and carried a purse. Interviewing Bowie in a hotel room, Mendelsohn was enchanted by Bowie's humor, roving intellect, and gift for self-promotion. He also admitted to developing a crush on him, though that night he would lose out to Bowie in a competition to bed a female groupie.

"He referred to pop music as the 'Pierrot medium,'" Mendelsohn later noted in a *Q* magazine Bowie special. "I hadn't a clue what he was on about. He seemed to have an extensive agenda and was happy to pose his own questions. He said something about being caught in bed with Raquel Welch's husband. . . . I suspect he thought it would make it into print and get him some attention. It made it into print—in *Rolling Stone*." It was while journalist and singer were visiting a radio station in San Jose that, according to Mendelsohn, Bowie first heard "I Wanna Be Your Dog" by Iggy Pop's group the Stooges. The song had a profound effect on Bowie, his radar ever attuned to the hip and unusual. By the time he returned to the UK a few days later, he'd already completed three new songs with heavy shades of both the Stooges and the Velvet Underground that would, in time, ensure his immortality: "Moonage Daydream," "Ziggy Stardust," and "Hang On to Yourself," the latter loosely demoed in Los Angeles with rocker Gene Vincent on backing vocals.

Back in London, the poor sales of "Holy Holy," issued as a single in January, provided further evidence that Bowie's career as a solo artist was all but dead in the water and that he should indeed concentrate on the role of backroom songwriter. For this purpose, he planned to create a fictitious group called Arnold Corns (after the Pink Floyd song "Arnold Layne"), to be fronted by Freddie Burretti, his flamboyant friend from El Sombrero. Arnold Corns—in reality a youthful trio called Rungk—set to work recording "Moonage Daydream" and "Hang On to Yourself" but encountered a major stumbling block: Burretti couldn't sing a note. This meant Bowie had to step in to record the vocals, but lame backing tracks did the songs few favors, and the resulting single barely registered on its release in May.

Meanwhile, Chrysalis, understandably eager for a return on their £5,000 investment, punted another new Bowie song to Herman's Hermits singer Peter Noone, then launching his solo career. His almost comically cheesy version of the future Bowie touchstone, "Oh! You Pretty Things," featuring Bowie on piano, reached No. 15 in May, at last vindicating Bob Grace's faith in Bowie's talent. Amid this flurry of activity, Philips finally released *The Man Who Sold the World* in Britain, with a different cover showing Bowie, resplendent in his favorite Mr. Fish man-dress, reclining like a wilting fin-de-siècle aesthete on the chaise longue at Haddon Hall. Bowie did virtually nothing to promote the year-old album except perform at a BBC live session in June. By then, with his Mercury contract due to expire, the game plan had dramatically changed. Recognizing the exceptional quality of his recent material, he decided to piece together a brand-new band to work on a new solo album. The group, soon to known as the Spiders from Mars, featured two familiar faces, Mick Ronson and Woody Woodmansey, plus yet another of their friends from Hull, bassist Trevor Bolder. All three moved into Haddon Hall, where Bowie and Angie were coping with another new occupant—their baby, Zowie Duncan Haywood Jones, born on May 30.

With this unusual domestic setup, the scene was set for the creation of two of the greatest and most influential albums in rock history—and the evocation of a fictional musical character who would become almost as famous as his creator.

The space oddity in his "space shirt," December 1969.

1971–1972
Leper Messiah

Before there was Ziggy Stardust, the flame-haired high priest of glam rock, there was "Ziggy Stardust" the song. When it was written, Bowie's Ziggy persona had yet to be created, as had the fictional band of the song's story, the Spiders from Mars. The Bowie who wrote "Ziggy Stardust" in the early months of 1971 still had long blond hair and favored Mr. Fish–designed man-dresses. But somewhere in Bowie's mind, the idea of blending his own personality with that of a fantastical rock star had taken root.

The formation of what would become Ziggy's backing group, the Spiders from Mars, occurred in early June 1971 as Bowie readied himself for a BBC Radio in-concert recording for *John Peel's Sunday Show*. A couple of days before the session, Bowie had phoned his estranged guitarist Mick Ronson at home in Hull and asked him to corral drummer Woody Woodmansey and a bassist—another veteran of the Hull rock scene, Trevor Bolder—and bring them down to Haddon Hall to rehearse. Ronson, licking his wounds after the failure of his group Ronno, jumped at the chance. So the three musicians, complemented by Bowie's old school friend George Underwood and former lover Dana Gillespie, assembled at London's Paris Cinema Studio to perform a set including several songs destined for Bowie's next album, *Hunky Dory*. These included "Kooks," an enchanting acoustic number inspired by the arrival of his new baby boy, Zowie (and written after a day spent listening to Neil Young's *After the Goldrush*), "Andy Warhol," and the hit he'd provided for Herman's Hermits' Peter Noone, "Oh! You Pretty Things."

In the pub afterward, Bowie—who hadn't performed with a band since the last Hype show a year earlier—was convinced the recording had been a disaster and that his career was over. But within days, he and the group were working at Trident in Soho on a new album with former Beatles engineer Ken Scott producing and Mick Ronson directing the musical arrangements. At a meeting at Scott's home, Bowie and

his publisher Bob Grace had decided on a track listing that favored acoustic- and piano-based songs over the singer's more rock-y numbers, which meant that the glam anthems "Ziggy Stardust," "Hang On to Yourself," "Star," and "Moonage Daydream" were set aside for future use. The plan was that *Hunky Dory*'s key tracks would be "Changes," "Oh! You Pretty Things," "Quicksand," and a remarkable song that had come into Bowie's head one afternoon while shoe shopping in Lewisham titled "Life on Mars?."

The notion that Bowie's stockpile of new material was strong enough to stretch over more than one album suggested a supreme new confidence in the singer's abilities, and indeed Bowie and manager Tony Defries were suddenly dreaming up grand schemes

Bowie and the Spiders from Mars give the first televised performance of "Starman" on the appropriately named *Lift-Off with Ayshea*. Bowie is flanked by bassist Trevor Bolder and guitarist Mick Ronson at ITV Studios, London, June 15, 1972.

Andy Warhol and one of his leading ladies attend a press conference to announce his new play, *Pork*, which premiered in the summer of 1971. Bowie's first meetings with the art icon were inauspicious, at best.

for Bowie's resurrected solo career, chief among them launching him in the United States. This wasn't as fanciful as it seemed: Defries was already scheduling a three-week US tour for Marc Bolan, who'd spent most of the year in the highest reaches of the UK charts with T. Rex. With Bowie's former record label, Philips, strong-armed out of the picture, Defries and his business partner Laurence Myers were funding the Trident sessions (and therefore owning the tapes) via their company Gem. By the end of July, there was enough material in the bag for Defries to fly to New York with a five-song acetate to court RCA Records, the American label that in the 1960s had grown into one of the world's biggest imprints thanks to Elvis Presley.

Two weeks into the *Hunky Dory* sessions, on June 23, Bowie appeared on his own at the Glastonbury Fayre, the precursor to today's Glastonbury Festival. Because of a curfew imposed the night before, Bowie's slot had been pushed to the next day, when he appeared at sunrise to play to a field of mainly sleeping hippies. His set, performed on keyboards and twelve-string acoustic, included "Kooks," which he introduced by explaining he was married to an American lady ("round of applause, please") who'd recently presented him with a son (already "three feet taller than I am"). He also previewed "Quicksand," "Changes," "Song for Bob Dylan," and "Oh! You Pretty Things," the latter hampered by a stage-invading Scandinavian girl tripping on acid, to whom Bowie quipped, "This is about the homo superior, love—you're letting the lyrics down badly." The set ended with a rousing rendition of "Memory of a Free Festival," by which time many of the sleeping revelers had stirred and were rewarding Bowie's efforts with a dawn chorus of rapturous applause. Moved by the ovation, he confided to his audience that he didn't do gigs anymore: "I got so pissed off with working and dying a death every time I worked . . . it's really nice to have somebody appreciate me for a change."

Bowie would soon discover he was appreciated in places he was completely unaware of. On August 2, the first UK production of the outrageous off-Broadway play *Pork* was staged at the Roundhouse. Inspired by Brigid Polk, one of Andy Warhol's starlets, it featured nudity, masturbation, transsexuality, and a wonderfully blank portrayal of Warhol by actor Tony Zanetta. The play was tailor-made for Angie and Bowie's outré tastes, though in a curious twist, several principal members of the

(opposite)
Bowie at the piano, Haddon Hall, spring 1971.

American cast were already Bowie fans, having been impressed by John Mendelsohn's account in *Rolling Stone* magazine of the dress-wearing singer's visit to the States earlier in the year.

Eager to meet him, three of *Pork*'s stars—Leee Childers, Kathy Dorritie, and Wayne County—cornered their quarry at a gig Bowie and Ronson were playing at the Country Club on Haverstock Hill, just up the road from the Roundhouse. At first, they found Bowie shy and unassuming and his gregarious wife far better company. But when invited back for a party at Haddon Hall, the charismatic David Bowie character they'd read about came to life, and they quickly fell under his spell—particularly Tony Zanetta, whose ability to bewitch those around him matched Bowie's own. Soon, the two men were fast friends, much to the bemusement of Ronson, who would remain

Bowie with his former girlfriend, Dana Gillespie, the actress and singer around the time she recorded vocals for the *Ziggy Stardust* LP.

uncomfortable with the attentions he received from the sexually unconventional American visitors. Bowie and Angie, however, were in their element, and the *Pork* cast's outlandish personalities excited Bowie's interest in creating a more outrageous persona for himself.

After the final touches were added to *Hunky Dory*, including Rick Wakeman's rococo piano parts, played on Trident's Bechstein piano (the very same one that Paul McCartney had used on "Hey Jude"), Defries flew back to New York in September for further meetings with RCA, this time with Bowie, Angie, and Ronson in tow. Defries's pitch to RCA was simple: Elvis, its biggest star, was no longer selling millions of records, and now, just as the Beatles had reshaped the 1960s, so David Bowie was poised to become the greatest artist of the 1970s. The proof may not have been evident in his record sales, but it was clearly apparent in the songs on *Hunky Dory* and in the man himself. David Katz, RCA's head of A&R, may not have entirely bought Defries's line, but he recognized Bowie's potential and signed him for a multi-album deal, with an immediate payment of $37,500 to secure the *Hunky Dory* tapes, and half that amount again as an advance against the next album Bowie delivered. RCA also paid for the right to re-release Bowie's two Philips long-players, which Defries had acquired from the singer's former label. According to Bowie biographers Peter and Leni Gillman, the deal resulted in a direct payment of £4,000 to Bowie, with a monthly salary of £400. Ronson, meanwhile, was to receive a wage of £30 a week, Bolder £20, and Woodmansey a mere £15.

The cover artwork for *Hunky Dory*, designed by Bowie's friend George Underwood.

While terms were finalized, Bowie was introduced to New York's cultural elite, beginning with Andy Warhol. The meeting was brokered by Tony Zanetta and took place at the Factory, then in the Decker Building at 33 Union Square West. Warhol frequently filmed his visitors, and footage exists of Bowie dressed in a Pierrot costume performing a mime routine for the artist. The famously poker-faced Warhol seemed unimpressed, however, though not to the degree he did when Bowie played him an acetate of "Andy Warhol," a song that gently satirized the mystique surrounding the icon and ended with a sleeping Warhol being sent away on a ship. Warhol responded by leaving the room. "He absolutely hated it," Bowie recalled in a BBC Radio interview in 1997. "He was cringing with embarrassment. I think he thought I really put him down in that song, and it really wasn't meant to be that." Warhol did, however, pay Bowie a compliment—on his bright yellow stack-heeled shoes, a present from Marc Bolan. But that was about it. "He had nothing to say," Bowie said. "Nothing at all."

As if to further connect the real world of Warhol's New York with the one he imagined, Bowie arranged to have lunch with Lou Reed at a restaurant called the Ginger Man near Lincoln Park. Reed had, of course, been a hero of Bowie's since he'd heard a pre-release disc of *The Velvet Underground & Nico* way back in 1967, and *Hunky Dory*'s

A pair of picture-disc editions of "Life on Mars?" which was released as a single at the peak of Bowie mania in 1973.

"Queen Bitch" was a brazen homage to Reed with its dirty guitars, neon-lit street poetry, and half-spoken vocals. Both men were cult artists destined for international success on the same record label, RCA, but in terms of their musical achievements, Reed was already a star and let Bowie know it. That same night Bowie, Defries, and Ronson—Angie was visiting her parents in Connecticut—went to the Factory set's favorite hangout, Max's Kansas City, where Bowie was introduced to another of his American inspirations: Jim Osterberg, alias Iggy of the Stooges.

After hearing the Stooges on his trip to the United States earlier in the year, Bowie had been smitten, and the band's dark metallic rock was a key ingredient in several

songs that took their final shape on his return to Britain in February, including "Moonage Daydream," "Hang On to Yourself," and "Ziggy Stardust." By the summer of 1971, the Stooges had disbanded and Iggy was a heroin addict, lodging at his former manager Danny Fields's apartment in Manhattan. When news came that an unknown skinny white English dude wanted to meet him, Iggy initially couldn't be bothered to drag himself away from the James Stewart movie he was a watching on TV. Eventually he did rouse himself, so Bowie was able at last to encounter in person the mythical rock 'n' roll miscreant he'd heard so much about. Though Iggy was in poor shape, his radiant charm remained undimmed, and Bowie invited him to take breakfast with him and Defries at the Warwick Hotel the following morning. By the time the coffee pots were empty and the plates cleared away, Defries was informing a dumbstruck Iggy that he would be signing him to his Gem production company, and that, once the singer had cleaned up, he would land him a new record deal (which he did, with Columbia).

According to some reports, amid all the madness, Bowie also managed to see his half-sister Kristina, who was living in New York after a spell in Canada. A late addition to *Hunky Dory* had been "The Bewlay Brothers," a haunting song

with a strange baroque vocal section and opaque lyrics in which Bowie again appeared to allude to his half-brother Terry, and his debilitating psychotic episodes. This he apparently played to Kristina as they discussed their upbringing and the schizophrenia that recurred in Bowie's mother's bloodline.

When Bowie's entourage returned to London, it took a while to take stock of what had happened. In their short time in New York, they'd landed a big advance from RCA, befriended Andy Warhol and Lou Reed, and brought Iggy into their fold. Defries's self-image as the ultimate cigar-chomping hustler was becoming a reality, while Bowie's confidence in himself as an artist was reaching an all-time high. Bedazzled by his own achievements, Defries took the step of appointing Tony Zanetta as his special representative in New York and employed former journalist Dai Davies as Bowie's publicist. With an ambitious business structure forming around him, Bowie unveiled his new band—featuring Ronson, Bolder, and Woodmansey—on September 25 at a gig at Friars, a venue in a market town of Aylesbury an hour or so outside London. For the past year, Bowie had submerged himself in the role of a stay-at-home songwriter, but Friars would mark—in his own mind, more than anything—the beginning of his transformation into a rock star. After extensive local promotion, around four hundred music fans paid 50 pence each to witness what was, to most of them, simply a show by a struggling artist who hadn't had a chart hit for two years or played live with a proper group for fifteen months. "We're going to start slowly till we get the hang of it," he told the audience, as he launched into a cover of American songwriter Biff Rose's "Fill Your Heart," the song which would open the second side of the yet-to-be-released *Hunky Dory*. By the end of the set (also featuring "Changes" and "Queen Bitch" and topped off with a rendition of the Velvet Underground's "Waiting for the Man"), the crowd was ecstatic.

"I'm going to be a huge rock star," he declared after the show to future music journalist Kris Needs, then sixteen years old. "Next time you see me I'll be totally different." Meanwhile, Tony Defries insisted that the promoter paid him in cash. "He was given the fee in 50p pieces," remembers Needs. "He went away, counted it again, then came back and said it was 50p short!"

Bowie was eager to record his next album, even though *Hunky Dory* wasn't scheduled for release until Christmas 1971. With the advance from RCA, money wasn't an issue, and after a month of rehearsals in Greenwich, Bowie and his band returned to Trident on November 8. Once again, Ken Scott manned the console, while Bowie seized control of the arrangements, to the extent of humming the solos he wanted Ronson to play. If *Hunky Dory* was to be Bowie's singer-songwriter album, the prevailing sound this time would be the noir-ish metallic rock that the Stooges and the Velvet Underground had invented—without either bands, conveniently, having made any impact on the mainstream UK (or, for that matter, American) charts. "I remember David coming in and

Bowie performing during the first run of *Ziggy Stardust* shows.

saying, 'You're not going to like this album,'" Scott told writer Mark Paytress. "I asked why, and he said, 'It's much more rock'n' roll' . . . I think by then he'd come to terms with the music industry. He wanted success more."

Much of what would become *The Rise and Fall of Ziggy Stardust and the Spiders from Mars* was committed to tape in the second and third weeks of November, with Ronson's flowing, liquid guitar playing, Bolder's busy bass runs, and Woodmansey's expressive flams the Spiders' defining elements. The straight rock setup meant the recordings were made quickly, and "Hang On to Yourself" and "Star" were nailed on the same day. "On *Hunky Dory*, each song was treated specifically to fit the way it was felt the song should go," said Scott. "For *Ziggy*, the basic sound was kept virtually the same for all the tracks."

On December 17, *Hunky Dory* was released in the UK, with the US edition following two weeks later. Brian Ward's front cover photo, colored by George

A posed portrait on the cusp of superstardom, April 1972.

Underwood, showed Bowie striking a pose inspired by screen goddess Marlene Dietrich, or possibly her rival, Greta Garbo. A repository for Bowie's quizzical meditations on everything from extra-terrestrial life to Nietzsche, fatherhood, silent Hollywood movie stars, art, and insanity, all set to some of the most beautiful melodies in rock, *Hunky Dory* was Bowie's first masterpiece. The voice that emanated from the record—that of a pleasantly kooky Englishman lost in his library of books, paintings, and old films—had the same cracked, bewitching allure as Syd Barrett's and a deep melancholia akin to the Kinks' finest work. "Changes," "Oh! You Pretty Things," and "Life on Mars?" contained all the drama of mini stage plays, wrapped up as they were in a pop-friendly format, while the kaleidoscope of cultural and philosophical references on "Quicksand" both celebrated and lampooned the beautiful, fathomless confusion of the postmodern hippie mind. The flipside of the album, with its accent on the United States ("Queen Bitch," "Andy Warhol," "Song for Bob Dylan"), showed a brilliance of another kind: gentle pastiche born of genuine admiration. Then there was the final comedown of "The Bewlay Brothers," with its disturbing image of a sibling lifeless on the rocks, possibly dead, possibly not.

Hunky Dory's greatness was not lost on the critics, with *Melody Maker* describing it as "the most inventive piece of songwriting to have appeared on record for a considerable time" and the *New York Times* proclaiming Bowie "the most intellectually brilliant man yet to choose the long-playing record as his medium of expression." These bouquets did not, however, translate into significant sales, with only two thousand copies shifting in the UK in its first month of release. Yet for Bowie, it was a triumph—"People [were] actually coming up to me and saying, 'Good album, good songs,'" he told *Uncut*'s Chris Roberts. "That hadn't happened to me before."

Bowie spent Christmas 1971 in Cyprus with Angie and Zowie before work restarted on *Ziggy* in early February. The final sessions of the album yielded versions of three songs that would dramatically change the shape of the record: "Starman," "Suffragette City," and "Rock 'n' Roll Suicide." Up until this point, *Ziggy* had not been conceived as a concept album per se, but now Bowie had a selection of material that could loosely tell the tale of his fictional rock star Ziggy Stardust, who becomes a messiah before falling foul of his own ego. The idea for Ziggy, Bowie once claimed, came to him in a dream, and though that may be true, when exactly he decided to adopt Ziggy as a stage persona is difficult to pinpoint. But it seems that by the end of January 1972 the process was well under way.

"Ziggy Stardust," the song, had been sketched out at a Holiday Inn in Los Angeles in February 1971 during Bowie's first promotional trip to the United States. Though the singer would later claim that the name "Ziggy" came from a tailor's shop, it also owed a clear debt to Iggy Pop, whom at that time Bowie had yet to meet. Ziggy's surname, on the other hand, came directly from cult American performer the Legendary Stardust Cowboy. "Mercury executive Ron Oberman took me to one side just before my departure from the States and furtively pressed a couple of singles in my hand," he informed the author in 2002. "'Play these,' he said. 'You will never be the same again.' Back home, I choked on [the song] 'Paralyzed' . . . and fell all about the floor at 'I Took a Trip on a Gemini Spaceship.' I became a lifelong fan and Ziggy got a surname." Ziggy's other key ingredient was leather-clad rock 'n' roller Vince Taylor, whom Bowie had befriended in the mid-1960s at La Gioconda on Denmark Street, and whose acid-fried mind had convinced him that UFOs were visiting Earth and that he was a disciple of Christ. From these components, the ultimate cosmic rocker, Ziggy Stardust, was born.

Though Bowie's creation still needed finessing, in January 1972 the singer moved a step closer to determining his physical form when Angie cut Bowie's hair short, the first time his ears had seen daylight since he'd appeared in *The Virgin Soldiers* in the autumn of 1968. The cut was refined shortly afterward by Ronson's future wife, Suzi Fussey, who feathered it on top while letting the back grow down Bowie's neck. Around the same time, the singer acquired a pair of wrestler's boots that laced up to the knee, and Angie and Freddie Burretti set to work at Haddon Hall on a series of glamorous, transgender costumes for Bowie and the Spiders from Mars to wear on stage. The look was designed to echo the image of Alex's gang of Droogs in Stanley Kubrick's recently released—and soon to be banned—film *A Clockwork Orange*, only here spangled with Bolan-style glitter. Brian Ward, who'd taken the cover shot for *Hunky Dory*, was enlisted to photograph the new-look group at his studio on Heddon Street in Mayfair. It was raining outside, so the Spiders opted not to pose in the street next to a red telephone box, though their leader did, creating the iconic early Ziggy images that would adorn the sleeve of Bowie's next album.

Ziggy Stardust and the Spiders from Mars, or at least a fledgling version, made its debut appearance at Friars Aylesbury on January 28, 1972, fulfilling Bowie's promise to journalist Kris Needs, made the previous September, that when he returned he would be "totally different." Certainly Brian May and Roger Taylor, attending that evening and looking for new ideas for their own band, Queen, thought so. "We loved it," recalled Taylor. "They looked like spacemen." In the dressing room after the show, the ecstatic mood was fueled by gate-crashing fans wanting to know where Bowie got his hair cut and bought his clothes. Pushing through the scrum outside to climb into his getaway car, Bowie was punched by an overzealous female admirer. "I think that was the moment Bowie realised it was really taking off," recalled the show's promoter David Stopps.

With the material for *Ziggy* in the can and *Hunky Dory* in the shops, Bowie set out on the promotional trail. On February 4, he and the band taped an appearance on the BBC rock show *The Old Grey Whistle Test*, performing "Oh! You Pretty Things," "Queen Bitch," and "Five Years," and giving their new sound and image their first national TV exposure. On February 10, they set out on a short nationwide tour that would eventually become a mammoth jaunt stretching until the end of the year. The first dates were given an invaluable PR boost by a revelatory interview Bowie gave to *Melody Maker* in January, in which Bowie claimed he was gay. The paper's Michael Watts had arrived at Gem's office on Regent Street to do a small piece acknowledging the release of *Hunky Dory* and to publicize the tour. Watts regarded the singer as "a swishy queen, a gorgeously effeminate boy" and felt compelled to enquire directly whether he was, in fact, gay. "I'm

Painting and decorating at his home, Haddon Hall, in April 1972.

(opposite)
An RCA Records promotional
photo showing Bowie in full
Ziggy getup.

gay," Bowie replied, "and always have been, even when I was David Jones." Bowie was being playful, though possibly calculated too, which Watts picked up on, telling his readers that "there's a sly jollity about how he says it, a secret smile at the corners of the mouth."

The quote had the desired effect: the story ran on the front cover of the January 23 edition, together with a photo of Bowie in a Liberty-print jumpsuit. In 1971 there were few, if any, openly gay rock stars (though plenty of closeted ones), and the statement was regarded as incendiary—though several readers affected outrage that the paper had fallen for such a blatant publicity stunt by an artist still widely regarded as a one-hit wonder. In 2002, talking to *MOJO* magazine, Bowie was candid about his motives. "I found I was able to get a lot of tension off my shoulders by almost 'outing' myself in the press in that way, in very early circumstances. So I wasn't going to get people crawling out of the woodwork saying, 'I'll tell you something about David Bowie you don't know.' I knew that at some point I was going to have to say something about my life. Ziggy enabled me to make things more comfortable for myself."

Bowie's tour initially comprised around twenty dates, beginning at the unremarkable setting of the Toby Jug pub in Tolworth, on the fringes of Southwest London. As few as twenty or thirty people attended the earliest shows, but with each one, Ziggy and the Spiders—who, as red-blooded Northern lads had to be coerced by Angie into wearing their brightly colored, revealing jumpsuits—grew in confidence. Angie played the role of stage manager, lighting technician, and catering manager, while Stuey George, a friend of Ronson's from Yorkshire, was appointed as Bowie's personal minder, ensuring the singer didn't come to any harm from over-enthusiastic fans or drunken homophobes. The group and entourage, traveling in two Jaguar cars, crisscrossed the country, gathering admirers wherever they went. Borrowing a trick from Iggy, Bowie often would launch himself onto the crowd in front of the stage, often with painful consequences when the concertgoers stepped aside. By the time they played at Manchester's Free Trade Hall on April 21, however, there were enough Ziggy-lovers to keep him aloft.

Manchester also marked another leap forward in Bowie's

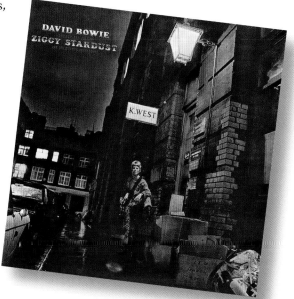

The cover art to Bowie's most famous album, *The Rise and Fall of Ziggy Stardust and the Spiders from Mars.*

assemblage of the Ziggy character: on Angie's instructions, Suzi Fussey had dyed his blond hair red. With Woodmansey painting "The Spiders" onto the skin of his bass drum, the difference between David Bowie and his backing band from Hull (augmented on these dates by keyboardist Nick Graham) and Ziggy Stardust and the Spiders from Mars was getting ever harder to discern. It was a conceit that Bowie increasingly relished. "It was a fun deceit," he told *MOJO*. "Who was David Bowie and who was Ziggy Stardust?" Ziggy, it would transpire, was a magnanimous being, for when in March Bowie heard that Island Records signings Mott the Hoople was thinking of splitting up, he proposed that the group record a new song he'd written, with a view to restoring their morale and propelling them onto the pop charts. The band was invited to hear Bowie play it on his acoustic guitar at Gem's offices, and so it was Mott, and not Bowie, that became synonymous with one of Bowie's finest compositions from the Ziggy period— "All the Young Dudes."

Amid all this frenzied activity, on June 6 *The Rise and Fall of Ziggy Stardust and the Spiders from Mars* hit the racks. For fans who'd heard some of its tracks performed

Mott the Hoople tears up London's Rainbow Theatre on November 14, 1971. Earlier in the year Bowie had gifted the band his song "All the Young Dudes," propelling them to stardom and likely saving their careers.

An early print ad for the album reveals "David Bowie Is Ziggy Stardust."

live, here at last was the album in full—and though Ziggy Stardust's story wasn't as cohesive as the title may have suggested, what the record's overarching narrative lacked in detail, the songs made up for in sheer panache. From the opening track, "Five Years," a swaying ballad predicting a half decade before the world ends, to the emotional, waltzing climax of "Rock 'n' Roll Suicide," it's an album big on melody and high on drama. And with tracks such as "Ziggy Stardust," "Star," "Lady Stardust" (a tribute to Marc Bolan), "Hang On to Yourself," "Moonage Daydream," and "Suffragette City," it became a touchstone for what was then dubbed "glitter rock" but would soon be universally known as "glam rock." If the album had a centerpiece, it was the timeless "Starman," a sing-along boogie with a yearning chorus melody lifted from "Somewhere Over the Rainbow" and an extraterrestrial theme that Bowie, still then best-known for "Space Oddity," was apparently monopolizing. The only incongruous piece in the jigsaw was "It Ain't Easy," a cover of a Ron Davies number that had been rejected from *Hunky Dory*'s track listing the previous year. Reaction from critics, perhaps still caught up in *Hunky Dory*'s sumptuous grooves, was curiously mixed. Michael Watts, who had posed the "gay" question earlier that year, found it "a little less instantly appealing" than its predecessor. *Cashbox* in the United States, meanwhile, called it "another example of the shining genius

On July 8, 1972, Lou Reed joined Bowie onstage at the Royal Festival Hall, London, to perform the Velvet Underground songs "White Light/White Heat," "I'm Waiting for the Man," and "Sweet Jane." A few weeks later, they proceeded to Trident Studios together to record Reed's breakthrough solo album, *Transformer (opposite)*.

of David Bowie." *NME* regarded it as evidence that Bowie was "tremendous."

During a short break in what was now becoming a never-ending tour, Bowie, Defries, and Ronson flew to New York to set up a string of US dates in the autumn. The evening they arrived, RCA took them to see Elvis at Madison Square Garden, where Bowie caught Presley's eye when the singer's entourage walked in late to take their front-of-stage seats, Bowie dressed in full Ziggy regalia. When the tour resumed, Bowie had a new trick up his sleeve, premiered at Oxford Town Hall on June 17. During the solo on "Suffragette City," Bowie danced over to Ronson, knelt down, and caressed the strings of Ronson's guitar with his mouth, thus simulating an act of fellatio entirely in keeping with Ziggy and the Spiders from Mars' intriguing sexual energy. The moment was captured on film by Mick Rock, who'd been recruited as Ziggy's official photographer. The shot—now one of the most iconic in rock—was distributed to the press, causing yet more ripples of delight/horror when it was printed. Among those most outraged were the citizens of Hull, who hurled abuse at Ronson's family in the street. The guitarist was so upset by the incident he declared he was quitting—and probably would have done so had Bowie and Angie not talked him out of it.

While "fellatio-gate" was erupting, Defries was hard at work empire-building. He had cut a deal with Laurence Myers, severing his ties with Gem and leaving him to manage Bowie's career alone. In return for $500,000 in deferred royalties, Gem would also surrender the masters of the four Bowie albums it owned. Defries called his new

management company MainMan, soon to become a byword for 1970s rock 'n' roll excess. Besides Bowie, his first signs were Iggy (now "Iggy Pop"), who since February 1972 had been living in London with guitarist James Williamson, writing new material, and Lou Reed, poised to record his first solo album for RCA.

The controversy regarding Bowie's bisexuality spread to the wider British public on July 6, when he performed "Starman" on *Top of the Pops*, the Thursday evening must-see BBC

An RCA Records promo EP, released in 1972, paired two tracks from *Ziggy Stardust* with two of Bowie's best-loved songs, "Space Oddity" and "Life on Mars."

music show. In a calculated move, Bowie sidled over to Ronson and casually put his arm around his shoulders, a gesture that in any other group might have suggested a touching matiness, but with the two men wearing makeup and dressed in tight-fitting, glittering one-piece costumes, the move communicated something far more risqué. The performance helped push "Starman" to No. 10 on the singles chart and Ziggy to No. 5. In the first summer of glam rock, with Slade on the charts with "Take Me Bak 'Ome" and Bolan rising high with "Metal Guru," Bowie had at last become the star he'd always dreamed of.

In preparation for the US tour that autumn, Defries flew a party of journalists over from the States to watch a return appearance by Bowie on July 15 at Friars Aylesbury, a venue where he was almost guaranteed a rapturous reception, followed the next day by a press conference at the Dorchester Hotel on Park Lane. Defries's new charges Iggy and Lou Reed were also in attendance at the junket, the latter having made an appearance the week before at a Save the Whale benefit concert at London's Royal Festival Hall, where Reed—clearly

The Ziggy songs would live long in the charts. Among the many singles released around the globe in the mid-'70s are this Japanese picture-disc edition of "Starman" from 1973 and a 1974 double A-side release of "Rock 'n' Roll Suicide" b/w "Quicksand." (opposite)

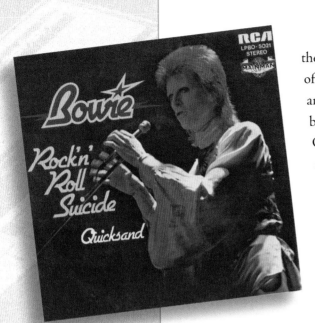

the worse for wear—had joined Bowie and the Spiders for an encore of Velvet Underground numbers. Later that month, Bowie, Angie, and the Spiders' rhythm section took advantage of a three-week break in the ongoing UK tour to fly to Cyprus for a short holiday. On the return journey, their plane flew through an electrical storm, badly shaking up the passengers—particularly Bowie, who from then on, partly out of genuine fear but also possibly to gain further publicity, decreed that he would never fly again. If the flight had proved turbulent, it was nothing compared to the tempestuous atmosphere the singer and Ronson encountered when they manned the mixing desk for Lou Reed's second solo album, *Transformer*, at Trident Studios that August. Reed's physical and mental state had deteriorated rapidly since they'd first met him in New York the previous summer, but somehow Bowie's simpatico approach to his hero managed to tease out some of the greatest music Reed ever made, including the tracks "Walk on the Wild Side," "Vicious," and "Satellite of Love."

Meanwhile, rehearsals for two prestigious Ziggy shows at London's three-thousand-capacity Rainbow Theatre were taking place. For these performances, Bowie roped in his old friend Lindsay Kemp to choreograph a troupe of dancers, while costumes were provided by the Japanese fashion designer Kansai Yamamoto. The production was a lavish affair, with a catwalk, ladders, and projections featuring images of twentieth-century icons including Marilyn Monroe, Andy Warhol, Elvis, Little Richard, and, during "Lady Stardust," Marc Bolan. With Bowie doing his man-in-glass-box mime routine during "The Width of a Circle," the show was an exhilarating fusion of dance, rock music, and theater, and opened with a set from Roxy Music, whose self-titled debut album had been released the previous month. The two nights were variously attended by celebrities including Warhol, Mick Jagger, Elton John, Alice Cooper, Rod Stewart, and Lou Reed (who had to be carried out horizontally by several MainMan employees).

A scaled-down version of the show was taken around the country for ten more dates before Bowie packed for his first-ever tour of the United States. The music critics of the world's greatest democracy were waiting for him, tantalized by the titillating stories of sexual excess and strangeness that MainMan's US publicist and former *Pork* star, Cherry Vanilla, had plied them with. And Bowie wasn't to disappoint them.

CHAPTER 4

1973–1974

Fame

(opposite)
Bowie onstage during the first night of US Ziggy Stardust tour, Cleveland Music Hall, September 22, 1972.

W hen David and Angie Bowie arrived in New York on the *Queen Elizabeth II* in September 17, 1972, tickets for the US leg of the Ziggy tour were selling, albeit very slowly. Bowie had yet to have a hit in the United States and for that matter had only released two successful singles in the UK—"Space Oddity" and "Starman"—but that didn't stop Tony Defries from behaving as if Bowie was the biggest British musical export since the Beatles. Instructing the singer and his entourage to "act and look like a million dollars," Defries proposed to dazzle the United States with an outrageous rock 'n' roll circus of a magnitude never experienced before. Deciding who exactly was financing the operation was a detail that Defries believed was best left until later—a contentious move with profound consequences in the months and years ahead.

Defries set up at office on East 58th Street, not far from the opulent Plaza Hotel near Central Park, where Bowie, band, and crew were all booked to stay. With only five days to go before the opening show in Cleveland, the Spiders had yet to find a keyboard player for the US dates but on RCA's recommendation auditioned Mike Garson, a Brooklyn jazz pianist, for the post. At a rehearsal at RCA's New York studios, Ronson asked him to play the chords to "Changes," and when he did so successfully, he was offered the job. Defries then summoned him to discuss terms; Garson suggested $800 a week, which the manager, eager to give the impression that money was no problem, readily agreed to. Little did Garson know that his wage was around ten times higher than the rest of the group's, with the highest paid, Ronson, still only on £30 a week.

The tour kicked off in Cleveland, where the local rock station, WMMS, had been playing *Ziggy* on rotation, and where a Bowie fanatic named Brian Kinchy had formed Bowie's first-ever US fan club. The 3,200-capacity venue sold out, and Bowie's debut appearance in the United States met with a rapturous reception and ended in a stage invasion. The next show in Memphis was also a sellout, after which Bowie and the band

The Stooges' Bowie-produced third album, *Raw Power*, recorded during the fall of 1972 and released the following February. Here, the Stooges are photographed backstage at West Hollywood's Whiskey A-Go-Go in October 1973. Clockwise from top left: Scott Thurston, Ron Asheton, James Williamson, Scott Asheton, and Iggy Pop.

dates and a poorly attended show in Kansas, where Bowie invited the 250-strong audience to the front of the stage while he performed cabaret-style, the tour reached Santa Monica. By then, Bowie's entourage had swollen to more than forty musicians, crew, MainMan staff, groupies, and hangers-on, including Iggy Pop, all of whom were checked into the sumptuous Beverly Hills Hotel, a popular—and expensive—hideaway for the Hollywood elite.

The visit quickly descended into a bacchanal, with even the roadies living off room service, champagne and steaks the sustenance of choice. The total charge came to around $20,000, a phenomenal sum, but with typical insouciance, Defries simply forwarded the bill to RCA, which in turn argued that the label had never agreed to underwrite the tour. Eventually, RCA agreed to settle the bill while a resolution was thrashed out. The Santa Monica shows—released as a live album in 2002—were another triumph, after which Bowie set to work at the Western Recorders studio mixing Iggy's debut album for Columbia, *Raw Power*. The job didn't take long, since, according to Bowie, only three of the twenty-four tracks available on the tape had been used. Iggy recalled Bowie was "uptight" at the mixing session, though the truth was that the singer's inability to differentiate himself from Ziggy was taking its toll. "I really did have doubts about my sanity," Bowie later admitted. "It was much easier for me to keep on with the Ziggy thing, off stage as well as on the stage." Iggy, meanwhile, was further rattled that the central character in "The Jean Genie" seemed to bear an uncanny resemblance to the ex-Stooge and felt that Bowie was using him.

When the tour moved on to San Francisco, Mick Rock was tasked with shooting a video for "The Jean Genie," which had been slated for a US release the following month. Bowie's latest UK single, "John, I'm Only Dancing," had been deemed too sexually ambiguous for the US market. Rock's footage included shots of Bowie outside the aptly named Mars Hotel, with Cyrinda Foxe camping it up as Marilyn Monroe. The tour was due to end on the West Coast, but Defries extended it through November, with Bowie sometimes playing to half-full venues and, in Nashville, suffering homophobic abuse. The road trip eventually ended with a four-night run at the Tower Theater in Philadelphia, soon to be a Bowie stronghold. Returning to New York, Bowie took the Spiders into the studio to record another song written on the road, "Drive-In Saturday," which, just as he had with "All the Young Dudes," he offered to Mott the Hoople, on tour in the United States at the time. When they told Bowie they weren't interested, in a fit of pique he got drunk and shaved off his eyebrows, though apparently not before he asked Angie to razor hers off first to see how it looked.

A posed portrait of the Spiders from Mars, taken around November 1972. From left: Mick Ronson, Trevor Bolder, David Bowie, and Woody Woodmansey.

The striking cover art to *Aladdin Sane*, devised by Bowie and photographer Brian Duffy.

Bowie returned to the UK in mid-December on the RHMS *Ellinis* to prepare for "homecoming" Christmas shows in London, Manchester, Glasgow, and a few other cities. He then booked Trident for a two-week stint in January to record his next album, *Aladdin Sane*. The experience of touring the United States had left a deep impression on Bowie, and not just in the images of the continent that would spill into the lyrics of songs such as "Cracked Actor," "Panic in Detroit," "Watch That Man," and "Lady Grinning Soul." Appearing on the *Russell Harty Plus Pop* chat show on January 17, 1973, Bowie looked ever more alien with his shaven eyebrows, pale skin, and large earring with dangling glass crystals. His attire, "a parody of a suit and tie" combination designed by Freddie Burretti, added to the spectacle of an otherworldly being.

The original candidate to produce the follow-up to *Ziggy* was Phil Spector, enjoying a career resurgence producing albums by ex-Beatles George Harrison and John Lennon. When Spector ignored MainMan's approach, the job went to the ever-dependable Ken Scott, who'd overseen *Hunky Dory* and *Ziggy*. Well drilled after a year's worth of solid touring, the Spiders worked quickly, though there were tensions between Bowie and Woodmansey when the drummer refused to play the straight Bo Diddley shuffle requested for "Panic in Detroit." Though the theatrical dynamics of "Time" were more ambitious than anything on *Hunky Dory*, the overriding style of the album was tough, Americanized rock, given a rich texture by Ken Fordham and Brian Wilshaw's sax playing and Mike Garson's piano. For the bewitching title track, Bowie asked Garson to draw on his avant-garde jazz background, which resulted in the song's hypnogogic solo of breathtaking magnificence.

On the record's sleeve, Bowie ascribed a location for each track, thus "Cracked Actor," with its opaque portrait of a drugged-up old Hollywood star, was Los Angeles, and "Drive-In Saturday" was assigned to Seattle and Phoenix. "Watch That Man," with its mad, sexually charged party scene, was attributed to New York. Around the time of the recording, storied British photographer Brian Duffy was commissioned to shoot the sleeve image: Bowie recruited makeup artist Pierre La Roche to create the iconic flash on the singer's face, inspired by the lightning streak on Elvis Presley's "Taking Care of Business" logo and representing Bowie's fractured psyche, caught as he was between Ziggy and David Jones. All the clues were there in the punning title: a lad insane.

The United States was calling again, but before Bowie and the band set off for a tour structured around multiple shows in the key music centers of New York, Philadelphia, Nashville, Memphis, Detroit, and Los Angeles, Defries had some serious ducking and diving to do. The powers at RCA were none too pleased with the $20,000 bill they'd been handed for the orgiastic Beverly Hills Hotel stay. Nor was the total tour deficit of a reported $100,000 looked upon lightly, especially since Bowie's total album sales in the country hadn't yet reached half a million copies, and that figure included the reissues of Bowie's Mercury album, retitled *Space Oddity*, and *The Man Who Sold the World*, as well as *Hunky Dory* and *Ziggy*. So much for Bowie being the new Beatles. But Defries remained defiant and cut a deal in which RCA, rather than MainMan, had to swallow the costs—though, of course, the money ultimately would be recouped from Bowie's future record sales.

Bowie and Angie set sail on January 20, 1973, on the SS *Canberra*, with the band due to catch up with them in New York. For this tour, the Spiders would be augmented by several musicians who'd contributed to the albums sessions, including sax players Fordham and Wilshaw, Bowie's old school friend Geoff MacCormack on backing vocals, and John Hutchinson from the Buzz and Feathers on rhythm guitar. Hutchinson's appointment was chiefly so Bowie could perform more freely onstage, without the

Bowie and teen fashion model Patty Clark at Union Station, Los Angeles, March 1973.

encumbrance of an instrument. While in New York, final overdubs were added to *Aladdin Sane* before the tour opened with two shows at the cavernous six-thousand-capacity Radio City Music Hall. Bowie made a grand entrance descending from the ceiling in a cage and changed costumes several times during the show. His wardrobe had again been designed by Yamamoto and included a white judo suit and black PVC onesie, while Pierre La Roche tended to his hair—now grown into a flame-red lion's mane—and makeup, replete with a white circle on his forehead. Once again, Bowie attracted a raft of famous faces, including Andy Warhol, Allen Ginsberg, and Salvador Dalí, who witnessed the unscripted finale of a stage-invader kissing the singer, who promptly fainted and was carried off stage.

Later at a night club, Bowie met black dancer Ava Cherry, who became his lover and was recruited as a backing singer for the tour—only to be informed a few days later that her services weren't required. Though Bowie and Angie tolerated each other's sexual dalliances, Bowie's friendships with Cherry and Cyrinda Foxe, and his wife's relationship with the Stooges' Scott Richardson, were beginning to undermine their marriage. Four weeks later, when the trip ended with two shows in Los Angeles and Bowie spent the night with a pair of notorious groupies, their "open" relationship was severely tested. There were other stresses, too, adding to the dark, druggy strangeness. Mike Garson, dubbed "Garson the Parson" by Bowie, was at that time a Scientologist and had succeeded in converting Woodmansey to the religion. Their friendship brought to light the ludicrous difference in their wages, which prompted the Spiders to mutiny. When they confronted Defries, he agreed to increase their pay to £200 a week but also managed to drive a wedge between them by offering to secure Ronson his own record contract.

In late March, Bowie's entourage sailed to Japan for a ten-day tour. The trip provided a sharp contrast to the chaos, bickering, and hedonism of the second US tour; instead of groupies, in Tokyo the Spiders were met by beautifully painted girls in traditional dress proffering flowers and gifts. Bowie instantly fell in love with the culture and attended Nogaku classical dramas and kabuki performances, as well as visited temples and moss gardens. It was during this time that he became enchanted by the right-wing writer Yukio Mishima, who'd committed hara-kiri after staging a failed coup attempt two years earlier. For the shows, Bowie was personally handed a new set of costumes by Yamamoto, including several kimonos and a white robe with his name embroidered in Japanese characters.

Bowie was reluctant to leave the country, but he needed to be back in London for a two-month UK tour starting on May 12. His method of journeying home was to prove exotic and illuminating. With Geoff MacCormack, Leee Black Childers, and American journalist Bob Musel along for company, Bowie took a boat to Nakhodka near Vladivostok and then boarded the Trans-Siberian Express for the six-thousand-

The *Ziggy Stardust* tour returns to Britain for the first-ever rock concert held at the eighteen-thousand-capacity Earls Court in London, May 12, 1973.

mile trip to Moscow. The journey through the alien landscape of Siberia and the steppes ended in the grim, colorless, oppressive cities of the Eastern Bloc, still bearing from the physical scars of World War II. The endless checkpoints, suspicious gazes, and needless paperwork gave Bowie firsthand experience of a totalitarian world that would find expression in his next batch of songs. When Bowie arrived home to London on May 4, *Aladdin Sane* was at No. 1 on the UK charts, and a huge crowd assembled to greet him at Victoria Station—though because he missed the boat train after a late night in Paris, his fans had to dash to his new destination, Charing Cross, to witness his arrival. The following evening, he and Angie threw a party at Haddon Hall, at which one of its estranged inhabitants, Tony Visconti, was a welcome guest. In another gesture of reconciliation, Bowie paid a visit to Ken Pitt, who was invited to the opening night of Bowie's UK tour at Earls Court.

The enormous Earls Court venue, usually used for trade shows and the like, had never hosted a rock show before, and the poor sound, seating arrangements, and facilities sparked a mini riot, forcing Bowie and the Spiders to leave the stage for several minutes while the promoters calmed down the tumult. Despite this inauspicious start, the Ziggy shows were about to reach their visual and musical apogee, wowing crowds with a rock 'n' roll show that assimilated elements of kabuki, mime, costume changes, and Bowie's Japanese-style costumes being ripped off to reveal his skinny body adorned with nothing more than a pair of red briefs. The rest of the tour, which stretched to some sixty performances in May and June, with the group sometimes playing two shows a day, wound up in London on July 2 and 3 for a two-night finale at London's Hammersmith Odeon. The second show was filmed by American documentary maker D. A. Pennebaker, who'd shot the Bob Dylan tour movie *Don't*

Look Back and *Monterey Pop*, which meant that arguably Bowie's most famous onstage moment was captured on celluloid. Before he closed the show with "Rock 'n' Roll Suicide," Bowie addressed the crowd, declaring, "Not only is it the last show of the tour, but it's the last show that we'll ever do."

News that this was Bowie's last-ever gig came as a complete surprise to the audience, but it came as an even bigger shock to Trevor Bolder and Woody Woodmansey, waiting in the shadows to play the last song of the set. The plan to kill off Ziggy, and Bowie's live career, had been hatched by the singer and Defries just a couple of weeks before, and only a few others, Ronson among them, were allowed in on the secret. Woodmansey in particular saw it as betrayal and typical of MainMan's underhand methods. At a glitzy party the following night at the Café Royal, where Mick Rock snapped Bowie, Lou Reed, and Mick Jagger enjoying a glass of wine together at the top table, the drummer was conspicuously absent. Meanwhile, Defries confirmed to the press that Bowie would, indeed, never perform live again—though the reasons why he unexpectedly "retired"

MAINMAN in association with MEL BUSH presents

★ **DAVID** ★
BOWIE
PERFORMING AS
ZIGGY STARDUST
HAMMERSMITH ODEON
45 QUEEN CAROLINE ST LONDON
TUES. JULY 3-1973 8.00 P.M.
TICKETS £1.50/£2.00

A promotional poster for the final Spiders from Mars show at the Hammersmith Odeon, London, July 3, 1973.

(opposite)
A candid shot of Bowie putting on his Ziggy makeup backstage, May 1973.

"The last show that we'll ever do": Ziggy makes his final live appearance, July 3, 1973.

Upon its 1973 re-release in the US, "Space Oddity" climbed to No. 15 on the Billboard singles chart.

DAVID BOWIE
SPACE ODDITY
THE MAN WHO SOLD THE WORLD

RCA
74-0876
A Mainman Artist

Ziggy were unexplained. And, since Bowie was no longer giving interviews to the press, they remained so.

The obvious motive was that Bowie was completely exhausted by his willing participation in the Ziggy Stardust fantasy, which had made him famous on both sides of the Atlantic but left him doubting his own sanity. Another was that he'd simply grown bored of the concept and wanted to move on to exploring his new Aladdin Sane character. There was also the suggestion that with Gary Glitter, Mud, Sweet, and others on the charts, what had glam rock become but a parody of itself? Yet there was another rationale, too, relating to RCA's huge investment in Bowie. Fearing it was getting only a modest return on its outlay—*Aladdin Sane* stalled at No. 17 on the US chart—the label was refusing to fund another US tour, scheduled for September. As MainMan didn't have the resources to put Bowie on the road again, it made sense to dramatically kill off Ziggy instead. As a footnote, the last shows at Hammersmith played a curious role in advancing the cause of British rock music. Local tearaway and budding rock star Steve Jones, then seventeen years old, crept into

(opposite)
Mick Ronson and Bowie at the Hammersmith Odeon. Though the guitarist didn't know it at the time, it would be his final show with Bowie.

Bowie and various celebrity friends—including Lulu, Jeff Beck, and Ringo Starr—celebrate Ziggy's retirement at the Café Royal, London, July 3, 1973.

the Odeon while Bowie's equipment was still on the stage and made off with several microphones and a Fender Twin amplifier. Thus the fledgling Sex Pistols nefariously acquired some decent equipment to help them on their way.

Just a week after the final Ziggy show, Bowie was back in the studio, though with a group that no longer included Woodmansey—sacked on his wedding day via a communication sent to Mike Garson, officiating at the marriage in his Church of Scientology capacity. The drummer's replacement was Aynsley Dunbar, who'd worked with Frank Zappa and, more recently, with Lou Reed. The group rendezvoused with Bowie at Château d'Hérouville, Chopin's former residence on the northwestern outskirts of Paris, which in the early 1970s had been turned into studio. (Bolan had recorded his *Tanx* album there the previous year and recommended it to his friend.) Bowie had

little new material, so the idea was to make an album of cover versions celebrating the songs he'd enjoyed listening to during his formative Mod period, 1964 to 1967, when he was an habitué of the Marquee Club. Among the tracks chosen were the Pretty Things' "Rosalyn," Pink Floyd's "See Emily Play," the Who's "I Can't Explain" and "Anyway, Anyhow, Anywhere," the Yardbirds' "Shapes of Things" and "I Wish You Would," and the Kinks' "Where Have All

Bowie with Lou Reed, Mick Jagger, and Lulu (standing) at Ziggy's party.

the Good Times Gone"—though it was the slinky soul version of the Merseys'"Sorrow" that Bowie truly made his own and provided him with a hit that summer. The album didn't pretend to be anything other than a stopgap while he recovered from the eighteen months he'd spent touring the world as Ziggy, but Bowie nevertheless approached the album with characteristic attention to detail. The cover, from a session rejected by *Vogue* magazine, featured the singer and 1960s icon Twiggy, made up by Pierre La Roche and beautifully photographed by Twiggy's then-partner, Justin de Villeneuve. Bowie even designed the back cover layout himself, choosing two of his favorite Mick Rock live pictures.

The original artwork for the third *Aladdin Sane* single, "Let's Spend the Night Together."

Released in October, *Pin Ups*, as it was called, gave Bowie his second UK No. 1, with a fraction of the work it had taken to get *Aladdin Sane* to reach the same position. But the fact that there was no longer a comprehensive tour of the United States that autumn meant MainMan had to come up with an imaginative way to keep Bowie in the American public's eye, and the answer came in a TV special commissioned by NBC for their *Midnight Special* rock slot. *The 1980 Floor Show*, as Bowie titled the production, was an extravagant affair for its time, filmed over three days in October. The location

Bowie kisses his wife goodbye at Victoria Station as he heads to Paris to record *Pin Ups*.

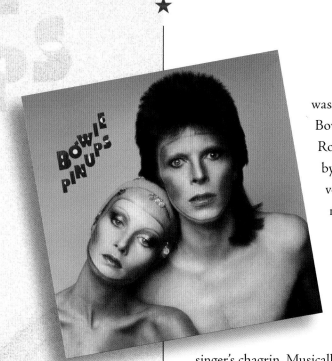

The cover artwork for *Pin Ups*, featuring Bowie and the British supermodel Twiggy.

was the Marquee Club—a nod to *Pin Ups'* inspiration—where Bowie assembled with a troupe of dancers and a group featuring Ronson, Bolder, Dunbar, MacCormack, and Garson, augmented by Arnold Corns guitarist Mark Pritchett and a trio of backing vocalists, including Ava Cherry. Much of the show's spectacle revolved around the high energy of Matt Mattox's choreography and Bowie's dramatic costume changes, ranging from a leotard with a large keyhole design—inspired by a similar garb seen in Tristan Tzara's Dadaist 1923 production of *La Coeur a Gaz*—to an extraordinary figure-hugging creation with giant fabric hands cupping Bowie's breasts. A third hand, holding his genitals, was unstitched on the producers' orders, much to the singer's chagrin. Musically, there was a genuine treat in the guise of a new song, "1984," a soul-disco-rock mutation unsuccessfully recorded for *Aladdin Sane*, and a superfluous turkey in Marianne Faithfull's tuneless duet with Bowie on Sonny and Cher's "I Got You Babe." Another guest was French actress, singer, and model Amanda Lear, with whom Bowie would have a romance.

The *1980 Floor Show* was broadcast in the States on November 16, by which time Bowie was planning two ambitious theatrical productions: a stage performance of *Ziggy*

Bowie and Marianne Faithfull, photographed during the recording of *The 1980 Floor Show* at the Marquee, London, October 20, 1973.

(opposite)
The Bowies—three-year-old Zowie, Angie, and David—at home in 1974.

Bowie and Ava Cherry watch from the wings as Rod Stewart and the Faces play a show on their US tour in March 1975.

Stardust, fleshing out the story with additional songs, and a musical of George Orwell's *1984*, for which, of course, he already had the title theme. The first idea quickly fell by the wayside, but the Orwell project progressed as far as *Pork* director Tony Ingrassia flying to London to sketch out a script, though Bowie soon lost interest. Its death knell was eventually sounded by Orwell's widow, Sonia, who refused permission for the stage adaptation—though not before Bowie had written several songs with an Orwellian theme.

Bowie and Angie were by now living on Oakley Street in ever-fashionable Chelsea, having moved out of Haddon Hall, which after *Ziggy* had become a mecca for rabid fans. (The future Boy George, then plain George O'Dowd and living in South London, recalled knocking on the door at Haddon Hall and Angie telling him to fuck off.) The Georgian house was close to Mick Jagger's home on Cheyne Walk, and the two singers become close friends and, according Angie, lovers (though some find this claim rather

fanciful). The Oakley Street address was opulently decorated, as befitted a successful rock star, with antique furniture, a Persian carpet costing £4,000, and pictures of Bowie's latest idol, James Dean. One of the couple's earliest visitors was novelist William Burroughs, taking part in an interview with Bowie for *Rolling Stone* magazine. Burroughs's work would influence a new song, "Sweet Thing," whose lyrics employed his cut-up method, a technique Bowie would continue to use on and off for the rest of his career. Another early visitor was Ava Cherry, whose presence Angie initially tolerated before it became clear that Cherry and David were getting a little too cozy; Cherry was soon relocated to her own flat nearby. At the time, Bowie was producing a session at Olympic studios in Barnes for the Astronettes, a vehicle he'd created to showcase Cherry's talent. The album, which was put on ice, included tracks Bowie would later revisit himself, though "Growing Up and I'm Fine," the superlative original he "gave" Ronson that year for the guitarist's

(opposite)
Bowie on the set of Dutch TV show *TopPop*, February 1974.

Bowie at the controls during the *Diamond Dogs* sessions at Trident Studios, London, 1974.

solo album *Slaughter on 10th Avenue*, would remain unrecorded by its creator except in demo form.

Ronson's new solo career spelt the end of his musical relationship with Bowie, leaving the singer without his trusty lieutenant when sessions for his next album, *Diamond Dogs*, began at Olympic in January 1974. Ronson's absence spurred Bowie to play lead guitar himself—which he did, with remarkable confidence—as well as synths and various other instruments, while Herbie Flowers was hired to play bass. The change of studio meant another key collaborator, producer Ken Scott, was missing too. He was replaced by the Rolling Stones' engineer Keith Harwood, who was later to achieve a curious kind of infamy when he fatally crashed at the same spot as Marc Bolan. The material Bowie had amassed related partly to the abandoned Orwell musical, as titles such as "1984," "Big Brother," and "We Are the Dead" attest. There were also hints of the aborted *Ziggy* play—"Rebel Rebel" and "Rock 'n' Roll With Me"—and a brand-new character, Halloween Jack, the star of the title track who "lived on top of Manhattan Chase" and led a Droog-like gang of feral, post-apocalyptic survivors, the titular Diamond Dogs. The album's dystopian, futuristic cityscape, filled with images of drug taking and homoerotic violence, was a disturbing place, reflecting a dark period that Bowie was entering in his private life. By now, his descent into cocaine addiction had begun, accelerated by the pressure heaped upon him to repeat the virtuosity of *Hunky Dory*, *Ziggy*, and *Aladdin Sane*. The destructive energy the drug unleashed was inherent in Bowie's stirring proclamation at the start of "Diamond Dogs," intoned over crowd noise lifted from the live Faces album *Coast to Coast*: "This ain't rock 'n' roll, this is genocide!"

Diamond Dogs' cover art, showing Bowie with a dog's body, was painted by Belgian artist Guy Peellaert from images of Bowie and an obliging canine taken by veteran 1960s photographer Terry O'Neill—though RCA insisted that the dog's genitals be airbrushed from the final version. The gatefold sleeve, nonetheless, retained a disturbed, deviant energy commensurate with its content, which Bowie viewed as

The *Diamond Dogs* LP cover, painted by the Belgian artist Guy Peellaert and featuring a half-human, half-canine Bowie.

A 1974 RCA Victor EP featuring UK Top 5 hit "Rebel Rebel," the lead single from *Diamond Dogs*.

A panoramic view of the *Diamond Dogs* tour, showing the extravagant "Hunger City" set.

"political" and looking back to the seismic upheavals of the 1960s and early 1970s. It was "my protest," he explained. But at the start of 1974, it wasn't just the demands of his art that were troubling the singer; there was also the gnawing realization that MainMan was spending his money almost as fast as he was making it. In New York, Defries had now set up an office on Park Avenue, where the staff had company credit cards and traveled in limousines. This beneficence did not, however, extend to settling the studio bills at Château d'Hérouville and Olympic, and as a result, *Diamond Dogs* was completed at Morgan Studios in North London and Ludolf in the Dutch town of Hilversum, where Bowie was booked to perform "Rebel Rebel," a UK hit that same month, on the Dutch TV show *TopPop*. Further tweaks were made at Tony Visconti's unfinished new studio in Hammersmith, for which Bowie bought some Habitat furniture as there was nowhere for him and the producer to sit.

Among others cognizant of MainMan's profligacy was a new recruit to its London office, Coco Schwab, an exotic French-American who would in time become Bowie's devoted longtime personal assistant. With the help of Schwab and Cherry, Bowie schemed to escape Britain—and possibly his relationship with Angie—and relocate to New York, where he could reinvent himself once more and keep a closer eye on MainMan's activities. But forensic scrutiny of his management's business methods may have seemed rather premature, because at his own behest, Bowie was about to embark on one of the most spectacularly expensive and financially ruinous tours of the mid-1970s.

Planning for the *Diamond Dogs* tour began in March, when choreographer Toni Basil was flown over to meet Bowie in London. Bowie was conceiving his return to playing live as an event that would astonish rock audiences as never before. On his birthday in January, Amanda Lear had taken him to see Fritz Lang's 1927 expressionist science-fiction epic *Metropolis*, which together with Robert Wiene's *The Cabinet of Doctor Caligari* planted the seed in Bowie's mind of staging a live show performed amid a giant cityscape, with shadowy skyscrapers, streets, gantries, and walkways. This would be Hunger City, the home of Halloween Jack and his Diamond Dogs. Set designer Mark Ravitz was given three "clues" by the singer to guide his blueprints: "power," "Nuremburg," and "*Metropolis*." There were to be dancers, special effects, and songs delivered from a cherry-picker raised up high above the crowd. MainMan set to work on a budget, which they estimated at $250,000, including the cost of transporting the set from city to city. The bad news was that, having had its fingers burnt by the *Ziggy* and *Aladdin Sane* tours, RCA refused point blank to finance the production, which meant ultimately the expense would be Bowie's own; with some imaginative accounting, Defries somehow made the figures work.

Bowie sailed to New York with friend and backing singer Geoff MacCormack— now styling himself "Warren Peace"—arriving on April 11. Booking into the luxury Sherry-Netherland hotel, the singer lost no time in exploring the city's nightlife with Ava Cherry as his guide. One of their first forays took them to the Harlem Apollo, where comedian Richard Pryor was a topping a bill featuring a funky soul group signed to RCA called the Main Ingredient. Bowie was thrilled by the show and to be the palest man in the building. The couple also became a regular at parties hosted by the wealthy art collector and socialite Norman Fisher, where guests were served cocaine in bowls.

Meanwhile, preparations continued for his ambitious stage show, for which Bowie still needed to enlist several key musicians. Short a guitarist, Bowie asked MainMan to contact his old associate from the Beckenham Arts Lab, Keith Christmas, who was sent a plane ticket to New York. "It was really exciting—though to this day I'm still not sure

(opposite)
Bowie reveals his new look during the Canadian leg of the *Diamond Dogs* tour.

why he asked me," Christmas told the author. "I arrived in New York and they put me up in a nice hotel, but I only had about a quid in my pocket. I had no money at all. So I went to MainMan's office the next morning and asked Tony Defries for some money, which was like asking Attila the Hun for some flowers. It wasn't a comfortable experience, but I got some. David and I went out clubbing, but the management were all over him like a rash, telling him he should be doing this or that."

At RCA's studio, Christmas was asked to play electric guitar on "Diamond Dogs," which he did repeatedly for thirty minutes or so. "The trouble with David was you never knew if he liked what you were doing or not. My guitar didn't sound very good, so after a while I said, 'How about a line then?' He started getting very paranoid, so we walked down these big corridors to the gents and he got out a packet of coke and an old-fashioned, double-sided Gillette razor blade. His hand was really shaking, so I steadied it. We went back and I played the riff again, adding in some notes in the last bar, and he said, 'That's good!' The session ended and I never heard from him again! I hung around a bit in New York, then flew home."

Also auditioning for the job was Carlos Alomar, a young New York session musician who, to Bowie's delight, had worked with James Brown and Chuck Berry. Alomar was firmly in the frame until Defries made it clear that he could only pay him $400 a week—half of what he was earning as a studio musician—so Alomar's future as one of Bowie's closest collaborators would have to wait. For a production of the scale he imagined, Bowie needed a musical director, whom he found when he attended a ballet production based on the life of the artist Auguste Rodin. Michael Kamen was a gifted composer who'd studied at the Juilliard School and, perhaps more relevantly, fused classical music and rock in a group called the New York Rock and Roll Ensemble. Kamen recommended a young guitar whiz, Earl Slick, who joined Mike Garson, Herbie Flowers, and drummer Tony Newman (who'd played on several *Diamond Dogs* tracks) to form the core of the touring band. The addition of two sax players, a percussionist, and a second backing vocalist made it the biggest group Bowie had fronted so far.

The band rehearsed for four weeks at RCA's studios, while *Diamond Dogs*, with its challenging mix of doomy synthesizer rock, Stones-y grooves, and nightmarish science-fiction imagery climbed to the Top 10 on both sides of the Atlantic. The omens seemed good—though the physical risk involved in staging the show were rammed home when the singer narrowly avoided injury after one of the walkways collapsed in the final dress rehearsals at Port Chester's Capitol Theatre. The extravaganza, unveiled to the paying public in Montreal on June 14, sent shockwaves rippling through the audience. First, Bowie no longer resembled the red-maned late-era Ziggy mutation of the *Diamond Dogs* sleeve; instead, his hair was cut into a fringe and he was kitted out in a dashing two-piece blue suit designed by Freddie Burretti. His new image owed a debt to the

(opposite)
To die, to sleep . . . Bowie channels his best Hamlet at the Universal Amphitheatre in Los Angeles, October 1974.

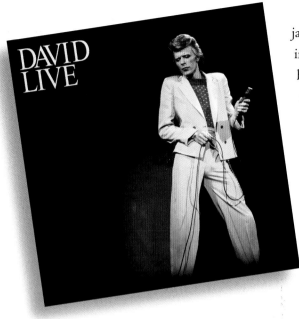

jazz musicians of the 1940s and had been influenced by Ava Cherry's description of her musician father's look as a young man in Chicago, when a broad silk tie and "gouster pants"—pegged trousers held up with suspenders—were all the rage. In fact, some of the items in Bowie's stage wardrobe were borrowed from Cherry's father.

But if Bowie's new image was a surprise, then the stage show was a seismic shock. Mock skyscrapers towered thirty feet high, gantries swung back and forth, and platforms rose and fell. Some of the technical aspects of the show were breathtaking and completely alien at that time to rock audiences. A cherry-picker floated Bowie above the audience for the "liftoff" sequence of "Space Oddity." During "Sweet Thing," the singer posed in a moodily lit street scene while dancers writhed as the Dogs; in "Cracked Actor," Bowie, suitably dressed in a Shakespearean doublet, addressed a skull. For "Panic in Detroit," Bowie sparred in a boxing ring with an invisible partner in time to the song's shuffling beat. After "Rock 'n' Roll Suicide," the show closed without an encore, only the dramatic announcement, "David Bowie has already left the building."

The reaction from the critics—and fans—was one of awe, with a local journalist frothing that it was "the most spectacular rock show I've ever seen." *Melody Maker* concluded the performance was "a combination of contemporary music and theatre that is several years ahead of its time," a view that few would have challenged. But the astonishing spectacle came at a price, and the thirty-two hours it took to erect the set using fifteen full-time roadies and twenty auxiliary stagehands meant that the production was subsequently scaled down. As the tour crossed North America, there were other difficulties, most comically Bowie being stranded high up on his cherry-picker for six songs after it malfunctioned and a truck containing the stage set ending up in swamp outside Tampa, Florida. But the biggest dramas related to Bowie's new backing group, who, much to their annoyance, performed throughout the tour behind black drape curtains so as not to detract from the dramatic scenery and intricately choreographed routines. There were also gripes about Bowie's drug-influenced mood swings, which resulted in sudden freezes and withdrawals. But the most spectacular fallout was over money.

The *David Live* LP, recorded during Bowie's run of shows at the Tower Theater on the outskirts of Philadelphia during the second week of July 1974.

The crunch occurred midway through a six-night stop at Philadelphia's Tower Theater—a Bowie hotspot if ever there was one—when it became apparent that the show was being recorded for a live album. When confronted, Defries offered each member the union rate of $70, sparking yet another mutiny among one of Bowie's bands. Flowers, acting as shop steward, informed Bowie that the group was going on strike and would not perform unless the fee was increased to an acceptable level—in this case, $5,000 per musician. With no other option than to pull the show, Defries acquiesced, though, typically, the group would not see the money for several years, and only then after taking legal action.

The resulting double-album, *David Live*, showed Bowie in transition between his glam-rock phase and his forthcoming infatuation with soul music, played by musicians fearing recriminations if they strayed from the script (a necessity of such a strictly choreographed show). New arrangements of some songs were not to everyone's taste, such as the supper-club treatments of "All the Young Dudes" and "The Jean Genie" and the ultra-melodramatic chanson rendition of "Rock 'n' Roll Suicide." When the first leg of the tour concluded with two nights at New York's Madison Square Garden on July 19 and 20, the touring party felt a sense of relief. So did Bowie, who already seemed to be tired of the constricting format and was restless to record a different genre of music that he'd become closer to via his relationship with Ava Cherry—soul.

CHAPTER 5

1 9 7 5 – 1 9 7 6

Cracked Actor

I n August 1974, a twenty-seven-year-old filmmaker named Alan Yentob was granted rare access to David Bowie to shoot a television documentary for the BBC. Screened five months later, *Cracked Actor* captured Bowie in the darkest days of his cocaine and amphetamine addiction. With skeletal features and translucent skin, Bowie looked desperately ill, though it was his distracted, twitchy behavior that was the clearest indicator of his enslavement to white powders. In later years, he would reiterate how painful he found the film to watch. But in Yentob's footage was a sequence where the singer looked surprisingly beaming, happy, and totally in control: in the studio, recording what would become the *Young Americans* album at Philadelphia's Sigma Sound Studios.

During a summer break in the *Diamond Dogs* tour at the end of July, Bowie traveled to Philadelphia to oversee a recording session by Ava Cherry. The location, Sigma Sound, was already a legend in soul circles; in the early 1970s, it was the preferred workplace for producers Gamble and Huff and their Philadelphia International label, whose stars included the O'Jays, Harold Melvin and the Blue Notes, and Billy Paul. Ever since Cherry had taken Bowie to the Harlem Apollo a few months earlier, the singer had become fascinated with contemporary black soul music and Afro-American culture. "Like most English who come over to America," he told *Q* magazine in 1990, "I was totally blown away by the fact blacks in America had their own culture, and it was positive and they were proud of it."

Bowie was particularly taken with Sigma Sound's house band, the MFSB, and declared his intention to work with them on his next album. As they were busy, except for their percussionist Larry Washington, Bowie instead called up Carlos Alomar and asked him to pull together a group of red-hot soul session players. The first recruit was Main Ingredient's drummer Andy Newmark, followed by Isley Brothers bassist Willie Weeks. The backing vocalists included Cherry, a then virtually unknown talent named Luther Vandross, and Alomar's wife, Robin Clark. The last key team member was Tony

(opposite)
The Gouster strikes a pose during the sixth of seven shows at Radio City Music Hall, November 2, 1974.

Visconti, who, though he'd mixed *Diamond Dogs* and *David Live*, hadn't produced a Bowie session since *The Man Who Sold the World* back in 1970. When Visconti arrived in Philadelphia in early August, the sessions were already underway, and the band and Bowie were in a groove. On the first evening with Visconti present, the extraordinary "Young Americans" was taped. The song was a perfect encapsulation of the joyous, sophisticated soul sound Bowie was chasing, complete with rousing gospel backing vocals, falsetto notes, and a jazzy sax riff. The lyrics, meanwhile, left the dark visions of *Diamond Dogs* behind for a bizarre and fractured story about lust, peppered with references to contemporary Americana—President Nixon, *Soul Train*, and cars such as the Mustang and Cadillac.

A poster advertising Bowie's weeklong stint at Radio City Music Hall as part of his "all new specular show."

In Yentob's footage of Bowie conducting the backing vocalists through "Right"—viewable in an extended form in the 2016 BBC documentary *Five Years*—he's animated, confident, and knows precisely what he wants, his instructions punctuated by an endearing, slightly nervous laugh. Visconti later described the two weeks at Sigma as "an extended jam," but nevertheless the foundation of *Young Americans* was laid down in this short period. The impressive work rate was aided by Bowie's coke-driven insomnia and reluctance to leave the studio when he did succumb to sleep. But while cocaine kept him working, it also made his voice hoarse, which would become a growing problem in the months ahead. Another difficulty was his relationship with Cherry, which made Angie's visit to Sigma a tempestuous event.

Bowie's change of style was a hit with the fans who gathered outside the studio each day—dubbed "the Sigma Kids"—but others weren't so taken with his change of direction. Defries was chief among them, but that wasn't the only reason that manager and client clashed that summer. With his new soul-man vibe, Bowie's extravagant, German expressionist–inspired Hunger City stage set suddenly seemed old hat. When the tour resumed with a residency at L.A.'s Universal Amphitheatre, it was reportedly only the presence of Alan Yentob's film crew that swayed Bowie to retain the expensive backdrop. Frustratingly, footage of the live performances in *Cracked Actor* reveal little of the set—though there's a sense of the show's grandeur in the footage of Bowie singing into a telephone receiver on "Space Oddity," high atop the moving cherry-picker.

The Los Angeles shows saw Bowie further embrace his "gouster" image, stunningly captured in the portraits that Terry O'Neill took of Bowie and actress Elizabeth Taylor around that time. The two icons had been guests at a party thrown for Dean Martin's son Ricci, attended by John Lennon, whom Bowie turned his back on—either in a coke-addled state, or in trepidation, or both—before retiring to another room. Meanwhile, the numerous music celebrities came along to see his performances, including Diana Ross and the Jackson Five, plus one of Bowie's oldest friends whose star he'd now sensationally eclipsed: Marc Bolan. Also invited was Iggy Pop, who a year after falling out with Bowie over the mix of *Raw Power*—which had stiffed on its release in February 1973—was no longer signed with MainMan and didn't have a record deal. Beaten up in the parking lot, he never made the show.

Yentob shadowed Bowie during a ride into the desert in car driven by the singer's new security man, Tony Mascia, a former sparring partner of Rocky Marciano. With his fedora, emaciated frame, and croaky old-fashioned London accent, the singer

An edgy Bowie plays with his cane during his appearance on *The Dick Cavett Show*, broadcast on December 5, 1974.

did indeed resemble a cracked actor, a dissolute thespian from Hollywood's golden age cocooned from, and not comprehending, the real world beyond his car's window. Yet Bowie had found a connection to the United States he saw passing by outside, which he reiterated to Yentob: soul music. As the tour progressed, Bowie gradually scaled down the Hunger City set and adapted the set list into what one critic described in November as a "soul revue." These autumn dates subsequently acquired the name the "Philly Dogs" tour, as Bowie's Halloween Jack character gave way to Bowie the soul man. Backstage, the peculiar collision of different cultures, drugs, and spiritual leanings created a strange atmosphere among the band. Meanwhile, Bowie was in parlous physical and mental shape, which his management's business dealings were making even worse. It had come to his attention that not only did he not own 50 percent of MainMan, as he had believed, but also the huge cost of touring *Diamond Dogs* was being deducted from his personal earnings. Any notion that he was a rich rock star was illusionary: the reality was that Bowie was fast heading toward bankruptcy.

The Gouster, the original version of what became *Young Americans*. Shelved in 1974, it finally saw release in 2016 as part of the *Who Can I Be Now?* box set.

Bowie's troubled state was communicated to the American public when he appeared on Dick Cavett's TV chat show "out of his gourd," as he later termed it, on cocaine. Dressed in a brown suit with padded shoulders, his orange hair slicked back from his forehead, he spent the interview stabbing insistently at the floor with a cane, clearly wired. There was no attempt, either, to disguise his continual sniffing. Cavett described the singer's backstage persona as that of "a working actor," to which Bowie smiled and commented, "Very good!" "I'm a person of diverse interests," he added. "I'm not very academic, but I glit [sic] from one thing to another a lot." (Asked by Cavett what "glit" meant, Bowie laughed that it was "like flit, but a '70s version".) Yet although he was stoned and his voice hoarse, the live versions he performed with his band of "1984" and "Young Americans" were polished and spirited.

When the tour returned to Philadelphia in late November, Bowie took the opportunity to record more tracks at Sigma, including a cover of Bruce Springsteen's "It's Hard to Be a Saint in the City." The Boss popped into the studio to say hello, completely freaking out Bowie, who, in his deranged state, found it impossible to make conversation with the songwriter. Following the final tour date in early December in Atlanta, after which police raided the wrap party at the Hyatt Regency Hotel, work on the new record continued at New York's Record Plant. These sessions produced the final versions of "Win" and "Fascination," which with "Somebody Up There Likes Me" and a new, funky version of "John, I'm Only Dancing," were added to the track listing for the album.

But *The Gouster*, as the album was titled, would soon be shelved, thanks to a string of events that followed a fateful and no less strange second meeting between Bowie and John Lennon. (*The Gouster* would eventually be reconstructed on the box set *Who Can I Be Now? (1974–1976)*, released in September 2016.) In his Bowie biography *David Bowie: Starman*, Paul Trynka reveals that Bowie invited Lennon and his girlfriend, May Pang, to hear a tape of the new album at his New York hotel room, but instead of just one former Beatle turning up, two arrived, as Paul McCartney was hanging out with Lennon at the time. Both ex-Beatles were impressed by what they heard but rather bemused that Bowie didn't play them any music other than his own. Not long afterward, in mid-January 1975, Lennon discovered that Bowie was recording a version of his Beatles song "Across the Universe" at Electric Lady. Intrigued, he paid the studio a visit, duly adding guitar and vocals to the track.

Then something momentous happened: Carlos Alomar was fiddling around with the riff to the Flares' "Foot Stompin'," which Lennon joined in with, singing "aaame," or something similar, at the beginning of every second bar. Accounts differ as to what precisely occurred, but within minutes Bowie had a new song called "Fame," skillfully layered onto tape that same day with drummer Dennis Davis and bassist Emir Ksasan. Much to his irritation, Visconti was in London that week, mixing the rest of the album and adding strings to "Who Can I Be Now?" and the incredible, imploring excursion into deep soul, "It's Gonna Be Me." When he returned to New York, Bowie explained that he wanted to drop "Who Can I Be Now?" and "It's Gonna Be Me" in favor of the two new tracks featuring John Lennon. Unsurprisingly, RCA didn't have any objections to the changes, aware of the benefits that a guest appearance by an ex-Beatle would bring to the project, though Visconti felt "sick" that the two orchestrated soul tracks had been discarded, especially for the stylistically ill-fitting "Across the Universe."

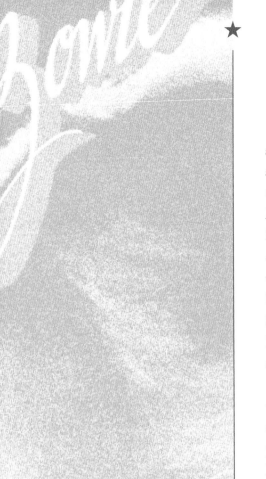

Bowie's ninth studio album, *Young Americans*, features a moody cover shot by Eric Stephen Jacobs.

The producer's grumbles were the least of Bowie's worries; by now, Bowie's relationship with Defries was all but over, and with the help of the ever-protective Coco Schwab, he'd commenced legal proceedings against MainMan via the L.A. lawyer Michael Lippman. Defries's reaction was to block the release of *Young Americans* (as the album was now called) until a settlement was reached. Bowie responded to the crisis by taking even more cocaine and hiding away in his first New York apartment, a brownstone on West 20th Street. Here his mood darkened further, and drug paranoia took hold, his blitzed imagination fizzing with UFOs, Nazis, ghosts, and the occult. Ava Cherry remembers strange happenings at the house, such as a glass mysteriously exploding in the singer's hand while discussing malevolent spirits.

With *Young Americans'* title track released as a single in February, RCA desperately needed the dispute between Bowie and Defries to be resolved. Such was the label's worry that Bowie's new music might never see the light of day that they arrived at Electric Lady to secure the tapes with a cash payment. The settlement, when it came, was brutal: MainMan would receive 16 percent of Bowie's royalties on everything he recorded for the next eight years and 50 percent from his existing back catalog. But at least his destiny was now his own; writing in *MOJO* in 2002, he was able to joke, "I left MainMan to it around 1975. Thank goodness somebody looked after [my money]. I'm sure I would have spent it on slap [makeup]. Or was that smack? No, David, it was coke."

In March, Bowie moved to Los Angeles, his soul credentials by then deemed impressive enough to present Aretha Franklin with Best Female Soul Singer at the Grammy Awards, though, much to his displeasure, she teased him for looking so ghastly. Afterward he hung out again with Lennon, photos of the occasion later shocking the singer—"I'm just a skeleton," he mused. But his fans hungrily embraced his new look and

Bowie, Yoko Ono, John Lennon, and Roberta Flack backstage at the 17th Annual Grammy Awards, March 1, 1975

radical excursion into "plastic soul" music. When *Young Americans*—with a cover portrait of Bowie taken the previous summer, moodily smoking a cigarette—was released on March 7, it climbed to No. 2 in the UK and No. 9 in the United States.

This time, though, there would be no tour to promote the album, which for fans in Britain (where he hadn't played live since Ziggy took his last bow at Hammersmith Odeon two years earlier) made him seem an even more mysterious and remote character. Instead, Bowie took a film role that would consume him for the next four months and take adjectives used to described him such as "mysterious" and "remote" to new levels of intensity. The movie in question was *The Man Who Fell to Earth*, based on the 1963 novel of the same name by Walter Tevis, and the director Nicolas Roeg, the British filmmaker who in 1968 made *Performance*, the cult acid-gangster movie starring Mick Jagger and Anita Pallenberg. The idea of casting Bowie in the lead role of Thomas Newton, a visitor from space in search of water for his dying planet, came from Jagger's film agent Maggie Abbott after Jagger himself was considered, then rejected, for the part. Abbott had seen *Cracked Actor* when it was screened on British television in January 1975 and immediately understood how Bowie could bring the necessary otherworldly magic to the role.

Bowie, meanwhile, was thrilled to revive the film acting ambitions he'd nursed since his bit part in *The Virgin Soldiers* half a decade earlier. Yet his life in Los Angeles that spring plummeted into a druggy daze, his only creative activity an aborted recording

A poster advertising the cinematic release of *The Man Who Fell to Earth* in March 1976.

session in May with Iggy Pop, who was in no better shape than Bowie. The two men had last met when Bowie had visited the Stooges frontman in an L.A. psychiatric hospital six months earlier, offering the patient a snort of cocaine as a get-well gift.

It was miraculous, then, that the eleven-week shoot that commenced in New Mexico in June passed without incident and, indeed, saw Bowie produce arguably his best-ever onscreen performance. Before filming began, Bowie had assured Roeg that he would steer clear of drugs, but later the singer claimed he was stoned throughout the process. If this was case, it certainly didn't harm his ability to learn his lines—one crew member recalled him being consistently word-perfect—or endure five hours in makeup for the scenes where he appeared in his natural alien form. Bowie regarded his detached performance as Newton as "not having to act," which to some extent may have been true, yet the way he moved and spoke onscreen was never less than compelling and convincing. As an emotionally remote alien who learns to enjoy the earthly pleasures of sex, booze, and ping-pong, he has yet to be bettered.

When he wasn't required on set, Bowie hung out with Geoff MacCormack, Coco Schwab, and his driver Tony Mascia, who appears in

Bowie and director Nicolas Roeg in Albuquerque, New Mexico, during the filming of *The Man Who Fell to Earth*.

A still from *The Man Who Fell to Earth* showing Bowie (as Thomas Jerome Newton) surrounded by television screens.

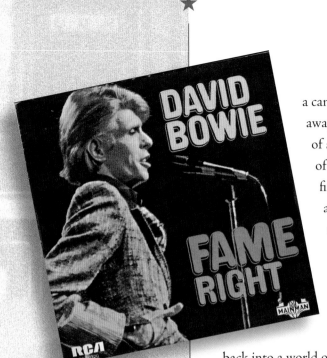

The single "Fame," Bowie's duet with John Lennon, gave him his first US No. 1.

A few months after "Fame" topped the US singles chart, a UK reissue of "Space Oddity" became Bowie's first British No. 1.

a cameo role as Newton's chauffeur. Besides UFO-spotting, he whiled away the downtime on location reading, painting, and writing a volume of short stories called *The Return of the Thin White Duke*. In many ways, of course, Newton and Bowie were the same thing—addicts who didn't fit into the conventional world, consummate actors, victims of external and internal forces they are unable to escape—so perhaps it was no surprise that when filming was finished, Bowie retained Newton's mannerisms, together with his slicked-back, red-and-blond hairstyle and beautifully tailored clothes, designed by Ola Hudson, mother of an eleven-year-old boy who'd one day grow up to be Slash from Guns 'N' Roses.

Back in Los Angeles, it didn't take long for Bowie to fall back into a world of drug dealers and leeches. It was also a period when his obsession with the occult became as all-consuming as the cocaine and speed he was ingesting in huge quantities. Before he'd left to film *The Man Who Fell to Earth*, a seventeen-year-old Cameron Crowe had interviewed him for *Rolling Stone* and lapped up stories involving witches, demons, and exorcisms. He noticed the blinds in Bowie's house were marked with runic symbols designed to ward off evil spirits. Aleister Crowley, namechecked in "Quicksand," was no longer a hip reference but an object of genuine fascination, his belief in "magick" as a third path between science and religion touching a nerve with the singer. By the time he'd returned to Los Angeles after filming, Bowie's interests had also widened to include the Judaic mystical teachings of the Kabbalah and the work of the Ahnenerbe, the Nazi archaeologists devoted to the search for the Holy Grail and the Ark of the Covenant, a subject explored in another text he devoured, Trevor Ravenscroft's *The Spear of Destiny*. Bowie would also spend hours glued to videos of old Nazi films, watching them repeatedly, high as a kite.

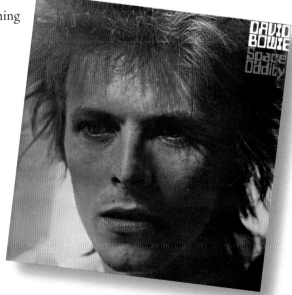

In August, Coco Schwab had found a rented house for the singer at 1349 Stone Canyon Road in Bel Air, a secluded 1950s-built property with a mock Egyptian interior. From here, Bowie pulled together a team to record his next album, for which he had only a couple of sketchy ideas. Harry Maslin, who'd worked on the "Across the Universe"/"Fame" session in New York, was recruited

as producer, while Carlos Alomar, Earl Slick, and Dennis Davis were joined by bassist
George Murray to form the core of the group. Mike Garson, who according to Bowie was
"off being a Scientologist" somewhere, was replaced by the E-Street Band's pianist Roy
Bittan. Warren Peace was also hired to help with Bowie's vocals.

After two weeks of rehearsals, the group entered Cherokee Studios in
Hollywood. Confidence was high: a few weeks before, "Fame" had gifted Bowie with his
first No. 1 single on the Billboard charts. Adding to the positive vibes was the knowledge
that, though he'd paid the price for severing his ties with MainMan, Bowie was no longer
an employee of Defries, nor did he have to worry where his earnings were being spent.
The jamming began, with Bowie promoting a spirit of "experimentation." One of the first
songs to emerge was "Golden Years," a sinuous soul groove that took up where *Young
Americans* had left off. It was premiered on November 4 on ABC TV's *Soul Train*, a
compliment indeed on Bowie's kudos within the soul community. Ever the perfectionist,
with the aid of cocaine and amphetamines, Bowie no longer needed to leave the studio
or, indeed, sleep. The drugs focused him to the extent that one session lasted twenty-six

Bowie clutches a carton of milk
outside Cherokee Studios, Los
Angeles, late 1975.

(opposite)
At the mixing desk during
the *Station to Station*
sessions, Cherokee Studios,
Los Angeles, 1975.

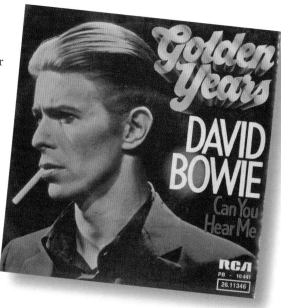

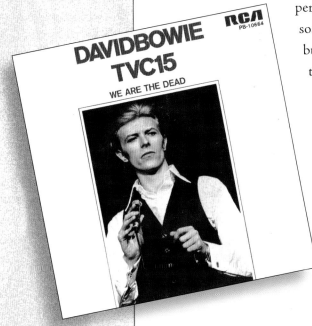

hours, at which point he was asked to leave the studio, as it had been booked by another artist. On a roll, Bowie simply moved the whole operation to the L.A. Record Plant nearby, and within a few hours they had resumed work on the track they were recording. After such superhuman bursts of activity, lasting three of four days, he'd then return to Stone Canyon Drive to rest. Surviving on a diet of milk and cocaine, with the odd vegetable thrown in, he outwardly seemed surprisingly healthy. Interviewed in November for the British TV show *Russell Harty Plus Pop* via a satellite link, he looked immaculate with his streaked Newton hair and possessed a deadpan humor and wit that effortlessly outsmarted his chummy host.

Though only six songs emerged from these sessions, they amounted to some of Bowie's finest work. The title of the book of short stories he'd begun during *The Man Who Fell to Earth*, *The Return of The Thin White Duke*, made its way into the opening line of "Station to Station," an epic eleven-minute piece that moved through a series of moods—sometimes dark, melancholy, and mysterious, elsewhere funky and euphoric—with allusions to the Kabbalah, cocaine, and, in its title, the Stations of the Cross, the popular representation of Christ journeying toward his crucifixion. In comparison, the beautiful "Word on a Wing" appeared to explore a more conventional Christian, or perhaps Buddhist, theme; "Stay" was a trippy funk-out with soaring psychedelic soul guitar; and "TVC 15" was a curious but catchy fusion of New Orleans piano and futuristic soul, telling the tale of a woman devoured by a television set. The final track, a cover of "Wild Is the Wind," the 1954 film theme memorably covered by Nina Simone in 1966, ended the album in a magnificently contemplative and dramatic style, completing a record exuding strangeness and imbued with layers of mystery. Bowie, however, later admitted he had few recollections of recording it, bar shouting his idea for a feedback part to Earl Slick.

Station to Station, as it was titled, captured Bowie in transition between American soul music and an art-rock aesthetic incorporating a new style of music being created in Europe: so-called "krautrock." Shades of the German groups Neu!, Faust, Tangerine Dream, and Kraftwerk could be heard in the pulsing introduction to "Station to Station," which prophetically talked of the "European canon," a body of art that suddenly seemed vital again after his excursion into black soul and funk. As soon as the album was finished, Bowie went back into Cherokee to record material for the soundtrack to *The Man Who Fell to Earth*, this time with multi-instrumentalist Paul Buckmaster, who'd played on *Space Oddity*, and pianist J. Peter Robinson. The group set to work using drum machines and synths to create mood pieces and mid-tempo rock instrumentals, but when the producers asked the singer to "submit" his work for scrutiny, he was so offended he told them he was keeping the recordings for himself. At the end of the sessions, exhausted after two years of relentless drug abuse,

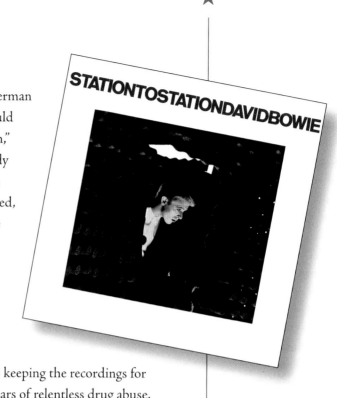

(opposite)
Bowie's tenth studio album in as many years, *Station to Station*, and the first of two albums to feature a still from *The Man Who Fell to Earth* on its cover.

(opposite)
A pensive portrait of Bowie as the Thin White Duke, taken shortly before the release of *Station to Station*.

A poster and program for the *Station to Station / Isolar—1976* tour, which kicked off in Vancouver on February 2, 1976.

Bowie collapsed on the studio floor. Buckmaster would admit in 2006 that, even though it was amazing, Bowie's score "wasn't really what Nic Roeg was looking for," and the soundtrack job was passed on to John Phillips of the Mamas and the Papas.

The rejection of the Bowie's score for *The Man Who Fell to Earth* was an unsettling end to an extraordinarily fertile year for Bowie, but there was more drama to come at Christmas. Unhappy with their relationship, Bowie unexpectedly sacked Michael Lippman, the lawyer who had become his manager after engineering Defries's departure. Locked away in his home on Stone Canyon Road, Bowie made the decision to take control of his life, starting with his drug addiction. The Bowie who emerged in January 1975 employed a personal trainer, was eating more healthily, and had scaled down his hedonistic habits dramatically. Some claim he even had even acquired a light suntan, though meeting him a few months later, the *Daily Mail* was nonetheless moved to comment he looked "terribly ill. Thin as a stick insect. And corpse pale."

continued on page 126

continued from page 123

(previous spread)
Bowie onstage at the Olympia
Stadium, Detroit, Michigan,
February 29, 1976.

The immediate reason for Bowie's new, comparatively clean-living act was that, after a year without touring, he was set to return to the road with one of his greatest-ever bands, one capable of blending all his diverse musical styles into a seamless, powerful new kind of rock.

Even the location of the rehearsals for the *Station to Station* tour signaled a salubrious change of scene. In January, Bowie summoned the core of his new studio band—Alomar, Murray, and Davis, plus Yes's keyboard player Tony Kaye—to Keith Richards's studio in the hills above Ocho Rios in Jamaica. Conspicuously absent was Earl Slick, who'd been caught in the crossfire between Bowie and Lippman, the manager having secured the guitarist a record deal with Capitol and unwittingly creating a conflict of interests. Slick's replacement was Stacey Heydon, a twenty-one-year-old who'd received a call at his girlfriend's apartment from Bowie's management, asking him to fly to Jamaica. (So fanciful was the idea that Bowie should contact him that his girlfriend hung up on the caller the first time they rang.) With only twenty-four hours' notice, Heydon had no time to learn any of Bowie's songs but nevertheless received the nod of approval after auditioning for forty-five minutes in what he described as "a pretty elaborate set-up at the top of this mountain."

The tour kicked off on February 2, 1976, at Vancouver's PNE Coliseum, where the audience witnessed a show that couldn't have contrasted more starkly with the mechanized extravaganza of the *Diamond Dogs* tour two years before. This time, the drama flowed from the bare black set, imaginatively lit with banks of white lights, and from Bowie's new stage persona, the Thin White Duke, whose wardrobe would settle into a monochrome vision of a Weimar cabaret artist—black trousers and waistcoat, crisp white shirt, and hair slicked back to his head. The austere European flavor of his image was underscored by the warmup tape, featuring Kraftwerk's *Radio-Activity* and a screening of Luis Buñuel and Salvador Dalí's classic Dadaist film *Un Chien Andalou* (in which an eyeball is dissected with a razorblade).

Along for the ride, though he never appeared on stage, was Iggy Pop. In the months since Bowie had visited him in hospital, Iggy had discharged himself and was sleeping rough. A mutual friend, Freddie Sessler, a concentration camp survivor and purveyor of fine pharmaceutical cocaine, had suggested he get in touch with Bowie, and a reunion took place in San Diego in January 1974. Almost immediately, Bowie floated the idea of making another album with the former Stooge, thus delivering him from a life as a bum. The two men got along so well that Bowie invited Iggy to accompany him throughout the *Station to Station* tour, making a pact that both would say away from hard drugs. The fact they stuck to their promise was borne out after a show at Rochester on

The police mug shot of Bowie taken following his arrest on drug charges in Rochester, New York, on March 25, 1976.

March 20, when police busted Bowie, Iggy, and two friends at the Flagship American Hotel and found only a small amount of marijuana. The charges were dropped, but the irony of Bowie's only drug arrest being for weed wasn't lost on the touring party. What the singer or his friends couldn't know at the time, though, was how breathtakingly cool Bowie looked in his police mugshots—flawless skin, chiseled jaw, perfectly combed hair—a fact that came to light thanks to copies of the photos appearing for sale on the Internet in 2007.

When the tour passed through Los Angeles, Bowie took the opportunity to pack up his rented house on Stone Canyon Road. At the after-party for one of the Inglewood Forum shows, the singer was introduced to Christopher Isherwood, then seventy-one, whose novel *Goodbye to Berlin*, based on his experience in prewar Germany, had been the inspiration for the musical and film *Cabaret*. It was while conversing with the novelist that Bowie first seriously considered the idea of moving to modern West Berlin, since 1945 an isolated Western enclave behind the Iron Curtain. Meanwhile, the rest of the North American leg of the tour continued attract rave reviews, and on hearing the *Live Nassau Coliseum* recording, an extra with the deluxe 2010 reissue of *Station to Station*, it's obvious why. Funky but also fluid and tough, the versions of new material ("Station to Station," "Word on a Wing," "Stay") and old ("Queen Bitch," "Five Years," "Rebel Rebel") worked together as a sensuous, stunning whole.

At the end of March, Bowie set sail with Schwab from New York to France, for what, unbelievably, would be his first-ever major concerts in mainland Europe. In Paris, he met his publisher at Chrysalis, Bob Grace, who asked how he'd managed to kick his coke habit. "I took that image off," he explained. "I put it in a wardrobe in an LA hotel room and locked the door." The tour began at Munich on April 7 and landed in Berlin three days later. After the performance at the Deutschlandhalle, he met Romy Haag, a fabulously beautiful transsexual who personified everything decadent and alluring about decaying 1970s Berlin and had opened the outré Chez Romy nightclub two years earlier. The two struck up an instant friendship, which would help convince Bowie that he'd found his new home.

After a show in Zurich, Switzerland, Bowie arranged a trip to Moscow to fill the week-long break before he was due to perform in Helsinki. With a small entourage including Iggy and Schwab, the singer journeyed by rail through Poland, marveling at the bleak beauty of the landscape still scarred by the Soviet Army's advance at the end of the war. Traveling on tourist visas, the party had no idea that they were being closely scrutinized until they were met by the KGB at the Russian border, which searched their belongings and confiscated several books Bowie was reading on the Third Reich. The visit to Moscow lasted only a few hours before they took a train to Helsinki.

The shows were a huge success, and the outpouring of affection for the once-distant star was overwhelming. But when Bowie made his dramatic arrival in London on May 2, the mood was suddenly to turn darker. While in Stockholm, Bowie had given an interview to a journalist in which he'd said, "I think Britain could benefit from a fascist leader." The comment followed dubious remarks he'd made to Cameron Crowe that had been printed earlier that year, including the claim, "I think I might have been a bloody good Hitler. I'd be an excellent dictator. Very eccentric and quite mad." He'd also likened Hitler's rallies to "a rock 'n' roll concert." In truth, there was little in the singer's quips to

(opposite)
Bowie gives a wave—interpreted by some to be a Nazi salute—from an open-top Mercedes at Victoria Station, London, May 2, 1976.

129 | CRACKED ACTOR

substantiate, or even suggest, he was a neo-Nazi, though an enduring fascination with the iconography and sinister magnetism of mid-century totalitarian regimes was patently clear.

Naturally, the British press chose to ignore any subtle nuances and concluded that Bowie was a Nazi. The matter exploded as soon as he arrived at London's Victoria Station, and he didn't help his cause much by standing in his touring vehicle, a black open-top Mercedes-Benz, looking suitably Teutonic and raising his arm to the crowd. Some primitive retouching to tidy up one picture resulted in what appeared to be a Nazi salute (though film footage shows it most certainly wasn't), supplying the press with all the ammunition it needed to crucify him as crypto-Fascist. Bowie reacted to the furor with genuine hurt, though it was also the wake-up call that stunned him into the realization that he was toying with dark forces. "It upsets me," he told Jean Rook of *The Express*. "Sinister I am not. What I'm doing is theatre, and only theatre."

Keyboard player Tony Kaye, Bowie, and guitarist Carlos Alomar during the first of six triumphant nights at the Empire Pool, Wembley, London, May 3, 1976.

Iggy Pop's Bowie-produced solo debut, *The Idiot*—a dry run for some of the ideas Bowie would explore on his own *Low*.

The audiences at London's Wembley Empire Pool arena had no doubts about the brilliance of the "theater" in question and gave Bowie an ecstatic homecoming reception over the six shows. It was then back to Brussels and Rotterdam before the tour wound up in Paris. With *Station to Station* now his biggest-selling album yet, reaching No. 3 in the United States and No. 5 in the UK and selling well throughout Europe, Bowie made good on his promise to record Iggy's next album. Bowie's original choice of location was Munich, but after a brief sojourn at Château d'Hérouville, where Bowie had made *Pin Ups* three years prior, it was decided to use the facility there. First, though, the singer visited the Swiss chateau Angie had found at Clos des Mésanges near Lausanne, which he didn't much care for, perhaps because it reminded him that he was still married though the couple had by now been living apart for almost two years.

Bowie returned to Paris and began work with Iggy on what would become *The Idiot*, starting with "Sister Midnight," a song he'd written with Carlos Alomar back in February and played to Iggy at the start of the tour. The rest of the material was fashioned in the studio with Bowie crafting most of the music and Iggy penning the lyrics, while the facility's manager Laurent "Tibo" Thibault added bass and Frenchman Michel Santangeli drums. Inspired by his European adventures and his interest in synthesizers, krautrock, and Brian Eno, *The Idiot* saw Bowie take yet another sonic left turn, this time into punk electronica—as if the Stooges in 1969 had discovered atmospheric guitar effects and synths. After the group moved the operation to Musicland Studios in Munich, the album was finished at Hansa Studio 1 in Berlin, with Alomar, Murray, and Davis overdubbing parts and producer Visconti, in his words, doing a "salvage job" on the tapes. Among the standout tracks were the classics "Nightclubbing" and "China Girl," both destined for bigger things at the hands of Grace Jones and Bowie in his 1980s pop period. "China Girl" was written about Iggy's brief relationship with Kuelan Nguyan, a Vietnamese woman staying at the Château, who would indeed tell the excitable Stooge to "Shhh . . . shut your mouth" and in general add to the atmosphere at d'Hérouville.

Bowie—who'd by now taken to smoking a briar pipe—was so knocked out by the album he decided to take its avant-garde electronic aesthetic and create his own record in that vein, putting his friend's album on ice to make it clear to the outside world who exactly was behind this exciting new sound. The era of Bowie's so-called "Berlin Trilogy" was underway.

CHAPTER 6

1977 – 1979
Subterraneans

Back in 1972, when Bowie, as Ziggy Stardust, performed at London's Rainbow Theatre, the support act was a new Island Records signing called Roxy Music. The story goes that Bowie wasn't overly thrilled by the arty, avant-garde glam-rock act's sudden success in the weeks leading up to the concerts and made a point of not speaking to them. But four years later, Bowie had become deeply curious about the solo career of its keyboard player Brian Eno, a musician who espoused a consciously theoretical approach to music over a practical one. Together with Berlin-born, British-raised artist Peter Schmidt, Eno had devised a pack of cards called *Oblique Strategies*, designed to help artists overcome writer's block and think laterally, with instructions such as, "What would your closest friend do?" or "Use an old idea." Just as intriguing for Bowie were Eno's latest albums, *Another Green World* and *Discreet Music*, which pioneered ambient electronic music and aimed to blend sound with environment so music didn't necessarily have the primary function of catching your attention.

After one of Bowie's *Station to Station* shows at Wembley's Empire Pool, the two men had fallen into a deep conversation, continued later that night at the house in Maida Vale where the singer was staying. Both admitted an admiration for the other's records, with Bowie revealing that the beautiful, palliating sounds of *Discreet Music* had been a constant companion while he and Iggy had been traveling across the United States and Europe. In the subsequent weeks, while Bowie was toiling away on *The Idiot* at Château d'Hérouville, he and Eno would enjoy long phone conversations about what music was and how it might be fashioned anew, which resulted in Bowie inviting the ex-Roxy conceptualist to contribute to his next album.

By the time Eno arrived at Château d'Hérouville, where Bowie had booked his own session in September, the musicians he'd assembled were already hard at work. Joining the Alomar-Murray-Davis core were Tony Visconti, veteran British rock 'n' roll pianist Roy Young, and guitarist Ricky Gardiner of prog rockers Beggars Opera.

(opposite)
**Bowie as Thomas Jerome Newton
in *The Man Who Fell to Earth*.**

Former Roxy Music multi-instrumentalist Brian Eno, photographed in 1976, shortly before he joined Bowie at the Chateau d'Herouville to begin work on *Low*.

(Tellingly, Bowie's original choice of guitarist was Neu!'s Klaus Dinger, but he declined.) Gardiner was Visconti's find, having impressed the producer with his mastery of effects pedals, while Young had to be tracked down to the bar of the Speakeasy Club in London. Sharing the same flight to Paris, Gardiner and Young polished off two bottles of spirits on the plane and were so drunk by the time they landed that they failed to find with Coco Schwab, who'd been dispatched to collect them.

The first days of the session before Eno arrived were willfully experimental and relied on the group cooking up riffs and passages of music from an idea or snatch of lyric that Bowie gave them. Alomar described their jobs as "plucking [the music] from the air." With Eno present, the unusual texture of the album began to take shape. The array of instruments that he and Bowie are credited as playing include ARP (an early synthesizer), Splinter mini-moog, "tape," "ambient sounds," and Chamberlin, an early electronic keyboard. By now only an occasional cocaine user, Bowie had instead developed an occasional thirst for strong alcohol. At one session, he asked Young to mix him gin and tonics from the pianist's supply kept under the piano; later, while Bowie was sitting lotus-like in the control room, listening to a playback, the others realized he'd passed out.

Among the songs to emerge prior to Eno's appearance were "Always Crashing in the Same Car," whose lyric paid homage to the beaten-up black Mercedes the singer was now attempting to sell, and "Sound and Vision," a smooth, undulating pop number that skillfully mixed soul, funk, and the crystalline, synthesized krautrock sounds emanating from Germany. Immediately after the backing track of the latter was nailed, Bowie rushed out of the control booth and sang the vocal part in its entirety. With the addition of backing vocals from Visconti's wife, singer Mary Hopkin, the song was complete. Another new number, "Breaking Glass," was inspired by Angie's unexpected visit to the Château with her new boyfriend Roy Martin. On the couple's arrival, Bowie suddenly became elusive, and when Martin sought out the singer to introduce himself, a noisy contretemps ensued behind closed doors. The tension between Bowie and Angie created a strained atmosphere, which made "Be My Wife"—a touchingly romantic entreaty from a lonely soul to his spouse—a curious track to emerge from the sessions. Estranged for two years, that autumn Bowie and Angie drifted away from each other for good.

Bowie's tendency at this time to fall into depression was reflected by *Low*'s title, suggesting the singer wasn't finding the escape from cocaine addiction nor the retreat from the fantasy worlds of his alter egos easy. Compounding his anxieties were the

Brothers in arms: Bowie and Iggy share a joke during the tour in support of *The Idiot*.

continuing legal ructions with his ex-manager Michael Lippman, whose representatives met the singer in Paris to try to tie up a severance deal. A conclusion to the negotiations was imperative, as Bowie's income from record sales and royalties had been frozen—in fact, the first check he'd written to pay for *The Idiot* sessions had bounced. The Château itself didn't lighten the mood either; Eno was certain the building was haunted and that he could feel the ghostly manifestation of previous famous occupants Frédéric Chopin and George Sand. There were also rumors of late-night Ouija sessions to try to contact those spirits and others. Back in the corporeal world, there were also clashes between Visconti and studio manager Thibault.

Eno's presence at the Château had its own dramatic effect. He had traveled to the sessions directly from Germany, where he'd been working with Harmonia, a group comprising Neu!'s Michael Rother and Cluster's Hans-Joachim Roedelius and Dieter Möbius. Tapes of this collaboration didn't surface until 1997, when they were released as *Tracks and Traces*, revealing a dreamlike affair with only one track featuring vocals. It was already Bowie's intention that *Low* should be a partly instrumental album, and after he played Eno and Visconti his abandoned *The Man Who Fell to Earth* soundtrack, the focus quickly switched to creating a series of evocative soundscapes. One of the tracks from Bowie's score became the basis of "Subterraneans," *Low*'s bleak, jazzy final track, on which Eno played his latest futuristic device, an EMS AKS suitcase synth. Their work done, Murray and Davis returned to the States, though not before Visconti had applied his state-of-the-art Eventide Harmonizer to Davis's snare drum, modulating its pitch without affecting the beat. Another instrumental, the funereal "Warszawa," grew from a series of notes Visconti's son had picked out on a keyboard and was shaped by Bowie to evoke the bleak train journey he'd taken through the Eastern Bloc with Iggy a few months earlier. Eno suggested adding a chant inspired by a recording he owned of a Balkan boys' choir.

Toward the end of September, when the album still carried the rather ostentatious working title *New Music: Night and Day*, Bowie, Iggy, Visconti, and Eno relocated to West Berlin, first staying in the Schlosshotel Gerhus and then taking a large apartment at 155 Hauptstrasse, an anonymous thoroughfare in the Schöneberg district of the city. Work resumed at Hansa 1 studio, where two new instrumentals were recorded, "Art Decade," on which the studio engineer Eduard Meyer added cello, and "Weeping Wall," a piece influenced by minimalist composer Philip Glass's use of repetitive phrasing, featuring Bowie playing every instrument himself.

Both "Art Decade" and "Weeping Wall" were hymns to a city in which Bowie immediately felt at home. For the first time in five years, he could walk the streets virtually unmolested and blend into the day-to-day life of Berliners without being paid special attention. "The whole reason for going there was because it was so low-key," he

Hansa Tonstudios Meistersaal, the former concert hall where Bowie and producer Tony Visconti put the finishing touches to *Low*.

told *Q* magazine's Adrian Deevoy in 1989. "Jim [Iggy Pop] and I—we were both having the same problems—I knew it was the kind of place where you walk around and really are left alone. They're very blasé there. Cynical, irony-based people, and it's a great place to do some soul-searching and find out what it is that you really want." Bowie had started to paint, a discipline he'd first briefly returned to during the filming of *The Man Who Fell to Earth*, and stopped dyeing his hair, which Visconti had cut short. His quest for anonymity also manifested itself in his dress sense: his deathly Thin White Duke image was replaced by the antistyle of blue jeans and a checked shirt, topped off with a rakish flat cap, though he still managed to look effortlessly cool.

"Art Decade" and "Weeping Wall" showed that Berlin stimulated Bowie in an unusual way, drawing out the bouts of sadness and despair that attended his recovery. Germany's history of expressionist art was, for him, a big part of the city's attraction, and he regularly viewed the collection of paintings by the Die Brücke group—Kirchner, Bleyl, Schmidt-Rottluff, and Heckel—displayed in a specially built museum in Berlin's western suburbs. But what really captured Bowie's imagination was the extraordinary nature of the city itself: located deep inside Communist territory, by the late 1970s West Berlin was depopulated, forgotten, economically depressed, and decaying, only existing because the West had resolved never to surrender it to the GDR. For Bowie, it was the perfect place for self-exile—and creating a new kind of existential music, with the Wall and its armed watchtower guards a constant reminder that the Cold War was very real and that life was a game of chance.

By November, *Low* was finished, with the final touches added at Hansa 2, a larger facility at Potsdamer Platz incorporating the Meistersaal, an elegant pre–World War I concert hall. The Meistersaal had an intriguing history, spanning its original use for chamber music recitals to a more sinister life as the location for Nazi dances to its postwar period as a venue for down-at-heel cabaret performances. When the Wall was erected in 1961, it passed directly behind the building, earning it the nickname "the hall by the Wall" when artists began using the facility in the 1970s.

Today, *Low* is regarded as one of Bowie's masterpieces and a crucial staging post in his development as an artist, but RCA's reaction to it was one of horror. Quite why the singer had chosen to make a half-instrumental album was lost on the company, as was the stately, sorrowful tone of much of the music. It was decided that the album should be bumped from the competitive Christmas schedule and instead be released in January, traditionally when less commercial or "difficult" albums appeared. Some sources state that Tony Defries, who still earned royalties from Bowie's releases, took steps to prevent the album from coming out at all, petitioning RCA to demand a more accessible record.

Ensconced in Berlin, Bowie refused to listen to the naysayers and prepared the cover artwork—as with *Station to Station*, a still of him taken on the set of *The Man Who Fell to Earth*. The use of an image that was now eighteen months old may have been construed as odd, but for Bowie it was making a point. Though he had conceded that the finished *The Man Who Fell to Earth* soundtrack complemented the onscreen story—it was pieced together from recordings by old artists such as Jim Reeves, Louis Armstrong, and Artie Shaw, plus John Phillips's and Stomu Yamashta's original material—he felt that *Low* represented what he'd been striving for but, in his coke-addled state, was unable to deliver. He sent a copy to Nic Roeg with a note that read, "This is what I wanted to do for the soundtrack." Roeg was deeply impressed, though some critics weren't so taken with Bowie's move into electronica. In *NME*, Charles Shaar Murray wrote that the album "stinks of artfully counterfeited spiritual defeat and emptiness." Nevertheless, fanfared by the peerless "Sound and Vision," *Low*'s highly personal fusion of soul, rock, and electronica was lapped up by fans, and despite little promotion, it made No. 2 on the UK charts and No. 11 in the States. Soon it would become the chief inspiration for the explosion of synth bands appearing in punk's wake.

In later years, Bowie would talk about *Low* in terms of "therapy," coinciding with his retreat from a rock-star lifestyle. Significantly, the album came out in January 1977,

Like its predecessor, *Station to Station*, *Low* featured a still from *The Man Who Fell to Earth* on its sleeve.

the same month the singer celebrated his thirtieth birthday in a Paris nightclub with Iggy, Schwab, and Romy Haag. Bowie could no longer pretend to be a young upstart, though compared with his peers—the Kinks, the Who, and the Stones—there was still something eternally youthful about him and his mission to continually challenge himself and his audience. And, in contrast to some of his 1960s contemporaries, his drug years had left few outward scars.

Berlin had revitalized Bowie artistically, but it also showed him that living quietly suited him, a realization that influenced his next move. In March 1977, Iggy Pop's *The Idiot* was released on RCA, and Bowie hatched a plan to help his friend promote it while still remaining resolutely in the shadows. The idea was simple: he would become the keyboard player in Iggy's band. RCA was understandably confused that Bowie was electing to publicize Iggy's record over his own, but the singer argued he wasn't ready to headline his own dates and knuckled down to organizing Iggy's tour. Rehearsals began in February at Berlin's UFA film studios, with Bowie putting together a group featuring Hunt and Tony Sales, the sons of comedian and Rat Pack associate Soupy Sales, who

Bowie and the dancer and nightclub manager Romy Haag at Alcazar, Paris, May 1976.

had been playing (drums and bass, respectively) in Todd Rundgren's band, and *Low*
guitarist Ricky Gardiner.

      The Sales brothers, then in their mid-twenties, injected a wildness into Bowie
and Iggy's Berlin existence that had previously laid dormant, and visits to sex bars and
nightclubs became a nightly event. The group having bonded in this old-fashioned style,
the tour opened in Britain on March 1 at the perennial Bowie stronghold of Friars
Aylesbury. Rumors that David Bowie was performing in Iggy Pop's band had persisted
in the press, but no one was sure whether the whispers were true, and promoters were
under strict instructions not to advertise Bowie's presence. On the afternoon of the
Friars show, one of the trucks full of equipment traveling from Berlin didn't arrive until
4:00 p.m., resulting in a few frayed nerves—though apparently not Bowie's. Journalist
Kris Needs remembered him seeming happy and relaxed in his flat cap, "milling around,
looking surprisingly healthy and oddly normal." During the show, Bowie barely looked
at the crowd, leaving the histrionics to Iggy, who hadn't played live in Britain since

Bowie looks out from behind the
keys during *The Idiot* tour's stop at
the Berkeley Community Theater,
April 13, 1977.

appearing at London's Scala cinema in June 1972. Among the audience was a celebrity punk contingent, including Johnny Thunders, the Damned's Brian James, and Glen Matlock, who'd recently left the Sex Pistols.

The presence of several punk icons underlined Iggy's status as the movement's godfather but also Bowie's unimpeachable credentials as an ultra-cool rock great. His Ziggy, Aladdin Sane, and Thin White Duke incarnations, not to mention his iconic role in *The Man Who Fell to Earth*, were written into UK punk's DNA, and *Low*'s out-there electronic stylings had done nothing to diminish his reputation as an innovator and outsider. In 1976 and 1977, Bowie was one of the few established British rock artists whom the punk elite didn't view as clapped-out or overblown. The Clash's Brixton-raised bassist and style icon, Paul Simonon, had once even been approached to act as a Bowie decoy.

The six-date UK tour—featuring songs from *The Idiot*, the Stooges' back catalog, and several new compositions destined for Iggy's next album—climaxed with two nights at London's Rainbow before moving on to North America, requiring Bowie to fly for the first time since his Ziggy days. In the States, the partying descended into scenes of debauchery worthy of Bowie's darkest days and temporarily made a mockery of Bowie and Iggy's attempt to stay relatively clean. Yet there were also periods of relative calm. Chris Stein, the founding member of Blondie, which was support on several dates, recalled to the author how "professional" both men were "and how accommodating. It was a momentous event in my career. Bowie didn't go out much, he stayed in his hotel, I don't know if he had a girl with him. There was a wonderful moment when me, [drummer] Clem Burke, [bassist] Gary Valentine, and Iggy went to the local punk house in Seattle. We went upstairs where all these kids were crashing, there were some amps and guitars, and we did 'Wild Thing' and 'I Wanna Be Your Dog' standing on a mattress.

Iggy Pop's second Bowie-helmed LP, *Lust for Life*, was released just five months after the first, *The Idiot*.

For years, people would come up and say they were there—maybe fifty actually were."

By the end of the tour, Bowie and Iggy's relationship was strained, with what Bowie later referred to as the "unbelievable" consumption of drugs a major contributing factor. Yet footage of the band performing on *The Dinah Shore Show* in Los Angeles on the penultimate day of touring reveals a musical unit in a suitably raw and committed state. When the tour finished, Bowie and Iggy returned to Berlin, where they quickly put the travails of the tour—and drugs—behind them and began work in Hansa 1 on what would become Iggy's solo masterwork, *Lust for Life*.

For the sessions, produced by Bowie, Iggy, and engineer Colin Thurston under the nom de guerre "The Bewlay Bros," Bowie used *The Idiot*'s touring band plus

Carlos Alomar on guitar and Warren Peace on backing vocals. The whole album was recorded at great speed—it took just over a week—partly because Bowie and Iggy wanted to spend as little money as possible on studio time so they could split what was left of the advance from RCA. The thunderous title track was, somewhat incredibly, written by Bowie on a ukulele, while mimicking the Morse code–like intro to the news on the American Forces Network TV channel, one of the few English-language stations available in West Berlin. "The Passenger," another highlight, was cooked up from a chord sequence that Ricky Gardiner chanced upon one day. In a process that Bowie would use to great effect on his next album, Iggy would often write lyrics on the spot, though the dark poetry of "The Passenger" and other tracks suggested that there was a great deal of craft involved too. Unlike *The Idiot*, whose release had been postponed until after Bowie's next album appeared, *Lust for Life* was rushed out in August at the height of Britain's interest in punk.

With Iggy's album in the bag, Bowie lost no time in assembling a band to record his own record. Dennis Davis and George Murray flew to Berlin to join Alomar, and together with Visconti they took rooms at the Gerhus at Bowie's own expense. Eno was invited too and joined Bowie at Hauptstrasse, while Iggy (who didn't play on the sessions) moved with his girlfriend Esther Friedman into the servants' quarters at the rear of the Hauptstrasse apartment. The experience of recording *Lust for Life* had impressed on Bowie just how quickly an album could be turned around if the musicians adhered to a strict regime, and conscious of the hotel bill he would soon receive, he encouraged a daily noon-to-eight work regimen to get the backing tracks in place as soon as possible. Each day began with Bowie eating raw eggs and Eno enjoying a bowl of cereal; the evenings, meanwhile, were spent at Romy Haag's nightclub and other lively hangouts, drinking in Berlin's decadent vibe.

Low had mostly been recorded in France, of course, so for Bowie's American rhythm section, the experience of working in West Berlin was a new one. Alomar, there for *The Idiot*, recalled a dislike of some of the local German men, whom he regarded as boorish and chauvinistic. This further hastened the desire to get the job over with as soon as possible. The group set up in the Meistersaal, helping Visconti produce the album's full, resonant sound. In contrast to Bowie's earliest albums, preceded by weeks of rehearsals and carefully charted arrangements, Bowie embarked on the "*Heroes*" sessions with a sketch of just one song, "Sons of the Silent Age," a dramatic but characteristically opaque meditation on Germany's

(opposite)
Robert Fripp, Brian Eno, and David Bowie during the *"Heroes"* sessions at Hansa Tonstudios, summer 1977.

A Spanish picture-disc edition of "Be My Wife," the second single drawn from *Low*.

Weimar youth, lifting lyrics from Jacques Brel, delivered with an eccentric Cockney vocal not that far removed from the songs on his 1967 debut album. For the rest of the material, a spontaneous methodology prevailed, sometimes incorporating jazz-style excursions into improvisation and "real-time" composition. The most spectacular of these experiments was the title track, "Heroes," graced by the almost preternatural talent of King Crimson guitarist Robert Fripp, a longtime ally of Eno's, who'd contributed guitar to *Another Green World* and, at the age of thirty-one, had considered himself "retired" from playing music. Fripp arrived in West Berlin jetlagged, but he immediately added a first-take guitar overdub to "Beauty and the Beast" that made it to the final mix. His contributions to "Heroes" were similarly extemporaneous; Visconti blended Fripp's three different "live" passes of lead guitar into the unsettling, transcendental sound that characterized the finished song. The guitarist's work was completed in a single six-hour session, after which he packed up his case and flew back to England.

One of Bowie's most enduring songs, "Heroes" would be released in numerous different editions—and recorded in various different languages.

On much of the album, Bowie had taken a page out of Iggy's book to create in-the-moment lyrics, and for "Heroes," he went so far as to record each new line as Visconti stopped and started the tape, a process that resulted in the song's strange, disconcerting story of two lovers, caught in an ephemeral but also eternal moment of bliss. Bowie was coy about his inspiration for the lovers "standing by The Wall," who "kissed, as though nothing could fall," though it was revealed after Visconti's separation from his wife Mary Hopkin that Bowie had glimpsed the producer and his then-secret paramour, backing singer Antonia Maass, canoodling under the gaze of the East German watchtower guards. The romantic image of love flowering in such a desolate, disquieting setting became central to the song's evergreen appeal, particularly so considering that, as with most of the other tracks, "Heroes" was initially conceived as an instrumental.

The Germanic influence on *"Heroes"* was clear; synths were more prominent than ever before, and Kraftwerk's Florian Schneider (and Hitler's last-gasp rocket bomb) were namechecked in the instrumental "V-2 Schneider." But once again, the Alomar-Murray-Davis axis imbued the music with an indelible funkiness, while on "Sons of the Silent Age," Bowie added liberal doses of jazzy sax to temper the floes of frosty, glacial electronica that characterized much of the album's second side, including the instrumentals "Sense of Doubt," "Moss Garden" (on which Bowie played a Japanese string instrument called a "koto"), and the somber, despondent "Neukoln," named for the area in West Berlin in which Turkish workers were billeted. "Sense of Doubt" and "Moss Garden" resulted directly from an *Oblique Strategies* session, with Eno and Bowie unaware of the instruction the other had picked.

After the rhythm section had finished its job and returned home, Bowie, Eno, and Visconti continued work on the record over the summer, finishing the final mixes at Mountain Studios in Montreux, not far from Bowie's Swiss retreat. The engineer at Mountain was David Richards, soon to become another regular Bowie collaborator, and his assistant Eugene Chaplin, son of comedian Charlie. *"Heroes"'* cover shot, taken by photographer Masayoshi Sukita, showed Bowie recreating Erich Heckel's 1917 portrait *Roquairol*—just as Iggy had mimicked the pose of the artist's *Young Man* for the sleeve of *The Idiot*. The reference to expressionist art was apt: a more complete and confident record than *Low*, *"Heroes"* was an album of stark contrasts and profound emotional depth, with a desolate tenor that reflected the extraordinary city in which it was created. "Berlin really captured, unlike anything else at that time, a sense of yearning for a future that we all knew would never come to pass," Bowie explained.

After taking a break in Spain, Bowie prepared for his first significant series of media interviews in nearly two years in advance of the album's release on October 14, 1977. Promotion got underway in September with an appearance on *Marc*, a British TV show hosted by his old friend and sparring partner, Marc Bolan, whose career had taken an unexpected upswing in the wake of punk. (As with Bowie and the Kinks, Bolan was never a target of punk hostility, and indeed that summer he'd hired the Damned to support him on tour.) But where once Bowie and Bolan had been equals, there was no longer any doubt as to who was top dog. *Marc* was filmed in Manchester, and for this, the final episode of the series, Bowie was due to mime to "Heroes," lifted from the album as its lead single. The mood was initially convivial, but Bolan suddenly flipped when he wasn't asked to play over Bowie's pre-recorded backing track. Then,

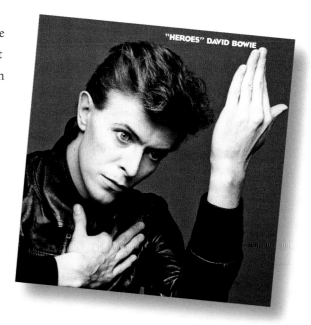

Bowie's "Heroes" LP, featuring a cover photograph inspired by the German expressionist Erich Heckel's *Roquairol*.

when Bowie's camera run-throughs were due to start, the studio doors were suddenly locked and everyone but the crew asked to leave.

Jeff Dexter, a club DJ and 1960s scenester who used to go UFO spotting with Bowie in 1968, found his path blocked by an unfamiliar security guard. "I barged past and discovered that some artist liaison guy at RCA had closed down the set," he told *Q*'s Johnny Black. Dexter sought out Bolan in the production office, only to find him rowing with Bowie over the fact Bowie's "people" were dictating the arrangements for his show. Dexter recalls that "it almost came to fisticuffs," with Bowie protesting he knew nothing about RCA's intervention. Things eventually simmered down and filming began, the

(opposite)
A lighthearted moment from Bowie's appearance on *Bing Crosby's Merrie Olde Christmas*, taped on September 9, 1977.

Bowie and Marc Bolan during a taping of the latter's British TV show *Marc*, September 5, 1977.

THERE IS OLD WAVE
THERE IS NEW WAVE
AND THERE'S
DAVID BOWIE

RCA

A striking print ad for Bowie's *"Heroes,"* and the *Peter and the Wolf* album he recorded, in part, as a Christmas gift to his six-year-old son.

program ending with Bowie jamming live with the host. That evening, Bowie and Bolan laughed off their spat over dinner in London, but they would never see each other again: nine days later, Marc Bolan died in a car crash, spookily driving into the same tree in Barnes that had claimed the life of *Diamond Dogs* engineer Keith Harwood two weeks earlier.

Four days after filming *Marc*, Bowie was back in a television studio again, this time at Elstree near London for the prerecording of a TV special, *Bing Crosby's Merrie Olde Christmas*. Bowie's appearance was primarily to mime to "Heroes"—with a new vocal take—but also involved a festive duet with the legendary American crooner, then in his seventies. The producers' choice was "Little Drummer Boy," but when he arrived, Bowie declared that he disliked the song and would prefer to sing something else. The show's musical supervisors, Ian Fraser and Larry Grossman, agreed to create a variation on the composition, miraculously knocking up "Peace on Earth" on a piano they found in the basement. Thus Bowie and Crosby duetted on what has subsequently become a much-loved Christmas staple, "Peace on Earth/Little Drummer Boy." Bowie found the recording "a bizarre experience," particularly as the ailing Crosby came across as if "there was no one at home at all"; in fact, Crosby died soon after his appearance with Bowie was filmed.

"Heroes" reached No. 3 in the UK but worryingly only made No. 35 in the States, where Bowie's sojourn in Berlin had removed him from the limelight—as, of course, was his intention. In Britain, meanwhile, a shrewd marketing campaign proclaimed, "There's New Wave, Old Wave, and there's David Bowie," reaffirming the singer's sanctity as rock's uber-cool one-of-a-kind. As to punk itself, Bowie would later admit that "it passed me by," an entirely believable comment considering his career trajectory in 1977, which ended with his narrating the children's story *Peter and the Wolf* for a recording featuring Prokofiev's magnificent score performed by the Philadelphia Philharmonic. Bowie considered the album, made in New York in December and released in May 1978, a Christmas gift to his son, Zowie, now six years old.

Christmas with Bowie, Iggy, and Coco Schwab in Berlin was a happy affair but triggered an angry reaction from Angie, who appeared in the British tabloid press peddling a dubious story about her husband having taken Zowie from the house in Switzerland without her permission. Soon after, Angie overdosed on sleeping pills but survived. These events effectively ended their marriage, and in January 1978, Bowie began divorce proceedings while preparing for his first major acting role since *The Man Who Fell to Earth*. The film, *Just a Gigolo*, was set in Germany at the end of World War I and directed by David Hemmings, star of the era-defining 1966 movie *Blow-Up*. Hemmings had enticed Bowie to take the part of a Prussian officer, who turns to prostitution, by coaxing German silent screen Marlene Dietrich out of retirement to play Baroness von Semering. Bowie looked undeniably amazing, whether in military uniform, black tie, or shabby cloth cap and coat, but the script proved poor, and worse, he and Dietrich didn't share any scenes together, though the film was cut to suggest they did.

While Bowie was filming, Schwab—now heading Bowie's Isolar management company—and RCA were organizing what would become the singer's biggest tour so far and occupy him for most of the year. It had been almost two years since he had played live, and the world was hungry to see an artist whose reclusion in Berlin had only added to his extraordinary mystique. Rehearsals began in Dallas in March, with a group that Bowie had hoped would feature Eno and Fripp. But as neither liked touring, the Alomar-Murray-Davis back line was instead augmented by Adrian Belew from Frank Zappa's band on guitar, Sean Mayes from Fumble on piano, and keyboardist Roger Powell, who'd recently played with Todd Rundgren's group Utopia. Bowie also hired violinist Simon House, whom he'd last encountered during his days hanging out with Hermione Farthingale back in 1968.

Carlos Alomar was put in charge of drilling the group in Dallas before Bowie arrived after a holiday with his son. The idea for the Isolar II dates, or the *Stage* tour as it became known, was to focus heavily on *Low* and *"Heroes"* and employ a striking but simple set featuring strips of fluorescent lights against a dark backdrop. Bowie's stylish outfits were designed by his old friend Natasha Korniloff, with whom he'd toured in Lindsay Kemp's *Pierrot in Turquoise* a decade earlier. The costumes were most memorable for the capacious pleated pantaloons that were soon copied by fashion outlets and marketed as "Bowie pants."

JUST A GIGOLO

DAVID BOWIE · SYDNE ROME

KIM NOVAK · DAVID HEMMINGS
MARIA SCHELL · CURT JÜRGENS
MARLENE DIETRICH

SCREENPLAY BY JOSHUA SINCLAIR
& ENNIO DE CONCINI

PRODUCED BY ROLF THIELE

DIRECTED BY DAVID HEMMINGS

ORIGINAL SOUNDTRACK ALBUM
THE MANHATTAN TRANSFER
MARLENE DIETRICH
PASADENA ROOF ORCHESTRA
THE RAGTIMERS PLUS ORIGINAL SCORE

NOW AVAILABLE AS A
CORGI BOOK WHEREVER
PAPER BACKS ARE SOLD.

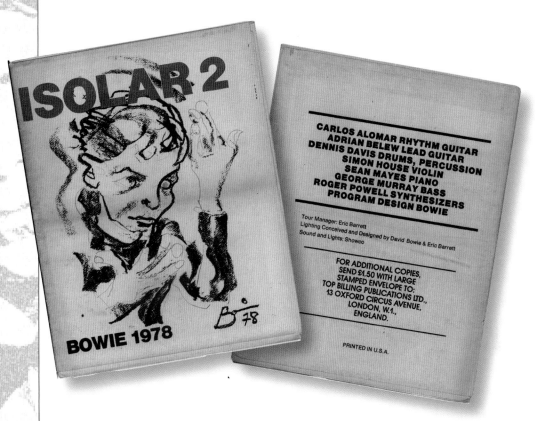

The front and back covers of the program for Bowie's first world tour in two years, which he dubbed *Isolar II*.

ISOLAR 2

BOWIE 1978

CARLOS ALOMAR RHYTHM GUITAR
ADRIAN BELEW LEAD GUITAR
DENNIS DAVIS DRUMS, PERCUSSION
SIMON HOUSE VIOLIN
SEAN MAYES PIANO
GEORGE MURRAY BASS
ROGER POWELL SYNTHESIZERS
PROGRAM DESIGN BOWIE

Tour Manager: Eric Barrett
Lighting Conceived and Designed by David Bowie & Eric Barrett
Sound and Lights: Showco

FOR ADDITIONAL COPIES,
SEND $1.50 WITH LARGE
STAMPED ENVELOPE TO:
TOP BILLING PUBLICATIONS LTD.,
13 OXFORD CIRCUS AVENUE,
LONDON, W.1.,
ENGLAND.

PRINTED IN U.S.A.

(opposite)
Bowie as Paul von Przygodski on the set of *Just a Gigolo* in Berlin.

A poster for *Just a Gigolo*, featuring Bowie alongside fellow stars Marlene Dietrich, Sydne Rome, Kim Novak, and Maria Schell.

The tour opened on March 29 at San Diego's Sports Arena in front of a crowd of around fifteen thousand, unsure quite what to expect. The stark, futuristic staging created an appropriate setting for Bowie's new synth-heavy sound, heralded by the opening number, "Warszawa," whose desolate tones still hung in the air as the strident opening bars of "Heroes" kicked in. During rehearsals, Bowie had decided, seemingly on a whim, that audiences should be treated to a seven-song suite of *Ziggy* material, to be played after a short interval to further intensify the unexpected pleasure of hearing highlights from his iconic breakthrough album. The group was requested to learn the whole record, from which Bowie settled on a shortlist of "Five Years," "Soul Love," "Star," "Hang On to Yourself," "Ziggy Stardust," "Suffragette City," and "Rock 'n' Roll Suicide." The reaction to the *Ziggy* numbers was euphoric, as was the reception for the whole show, which ended with a stunningly funky version of "Sound and Vision." Such was the buzz that, when the group returned to their hotel after the show, they jammed together in the bar before Bowie suffered a brief relapse in his attempt to stay off cocaine and embarked on an all-night bender.

The tour incited tumultuous scenes at every stop, including a two-night stand in Detroit where Bowie remonstrated with over-enthusiastic security staff and a barrage of gifts was thrown on the stage. The Dallas show on April 10 was filmed for a TV special titled *David Bowie On Stage*, featuring six songs including "Hang On to Yourself" and "Ziggy Stardust" from the *Ziggy* section. In Toronto, Bowie's path crossed with Lindsay

Kemp, touring *Salomé*. Such was the demand for guest passes at New York's Madison Square Garden that Andy Warhol was only sent a single pair. Afterwards Bowie and his entourage celebrated at the era's hottest nightspots, Hurrah and Studio 54. RCA was eager for another Bowie live record, and Visconti was dispatched to record the shows in Philadelphia, Providence, and Boston. Behind the scenes, a row brewed between Bowie and his label about whether a double live album would count as two discs or one, as the singer desperately maneuvered to fulfill his contract and move on to a new deal.

On May 14, the tour arrived in Germany before visiting Austria and France. Two weeks later, the group recorded a set for Bremen Radio's music TV program *Musikladen Extra*, which captured the essence of the *Stage* performance: Bowie sporting chic futuristic garb and playing a keyboard on "Sense of Doubt," Belew in a trademark

(opposite)
Bowie onstage at the Fresno Convention Center, April 2, 1978— the third date of the *Isolar II* tour.

Bowie and his band at Earls Court, London, August 28, 1978. From left: Simon House, Carlos Alomar, Dennis Davis, Bowie, George Murray, and Adrian Belew.

Hawaiian shirt teasing squealing notes from his guitar rig, Mayes and Powell creating dynamic interactions between piano and keyboards, and House adding further atmospheric textures with a violin treated with effects. Meanwhile, Alomar, Murray, and Davis were as funky as ever. The tour continued in Scandinavia and then Holland and Belgium, ending in the UK with three shows at the eighteen-thousand-capacity Earls Court Arena, the site of the disastrous *Ziggy*-era show five years earlier, though this time the sellout performances were a triumph. The gigs were filmed by David Hemmings, but as with *Just a Gigolo*, Bowie wasn't overly impressed with the results and vetoed the idea of releasing them as an official document of the tour.

Bowie's performances proved he was still an innovator, agitator, and master of his art, but also a maverick, and his hero status among the new rock elite was cemented on the eve of the UK dates, when he turned up to see Iggy Pop performing at the Music Machine in Camden and then went for a drink afterward with the ex-Stooge and Johnny Rotten. The impact of the tour—and *Low* and *"Heroes"*—on Britain's post-punk scene was proving seismic as the multitude of synthesizer groups that were forming across the country attested. Bowie himself also felt inspired by his performances, and on July 2, the day after the last Earls Court show, he arranged for the group to meet at Tony Visconti's Good Earth Studios in London to record "Alabama Song," the Brecht-Weill collaboration that now featured in the *Stage* set.

The *Stage* LP, recorded at various dates on the US leg of the *Isolar II* tour, opens with live takes of five tracks from *Ziggy Stardust* before turning to Bowie's recent output for the remainder of the two-disc set.

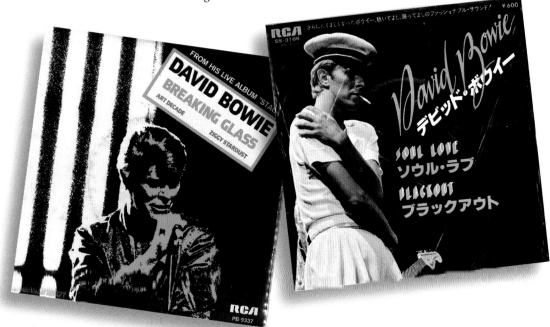

A pair of picture-disc singles taken from *Stage*, both of which pair tracks from Bowie's recent Berlin-era recordings with a song from *Ziggy Stardust*.

The third, final, and least well-loved entry in the so-called "Berlin trilogy," *Lodger*.

After a summer break, the band reconvened in September at Mountain Studios in Montreux to begin work on Bowie's next studio album. Although *Lodger* is regarded as the last in the Berlin Trilogy, none of it was actually recorded in Germany, but the presence of Brian Eno and his unorthodox methodologies make it an instantly recognizable companion piece to *Low* and *"Heroes"*. The initial sessions began, as was customary, with Alomar, Murray, and Davis creating the basic tracks, which at one point involved Eno directing their efforts by pointing randomly at a list of chords (an exercise Alomar in particular felt was a rather wearisome). On what would eventually become "Boys Keep Swinging," Eno asked the rhythm section to swap instruments, resulting in Alomar's primitive, propulsive drum beat and a quirky bass line by Davis that ultimately had to be overdubbed by Visconti. Eno's influence was also evident on the eccentric time signatures and world music inflections of "African Night Flight" and the Eastern-reggae hybrid "Yassassin."

Two picture-disc singles drawn from *Lodger*: "Boys Keep Swinging" and the Turkish-themed "Yassassin."

When the other musicians arrived, the experimental vibe continued, adhering to a philosophy inherent in the album's working title, *Planned Accidents*. Belew was presented with the same challenge that Fripp had encountered at Hansa, with instructions to play along with a track without first knowing the chords or even the key. After three passes, his work was considered done, since he would by then be too familiar with the backing track for contribution to be spontaneous. This method produced particularly effective results on "Red Sails" but eluded the guitarist other tracks, wherein more conventional methods were applied. At the end of the session, Bowie still hadn't committed any vocals to tape and indeed wouldn't do so for another five months or so when recording resumed in New York.

With *Stage* appearing at the end of September, the group readied themselves for the final leg of the tour, which would take Bowie to Australia and New Zealand—his first visits to those territories—plus a return visit to Japan. The Australian dates, beginning at Adelaide's Oval Cricket Ground, took place outdoors and, depending on the nature of each venue, attracted between twenty thousand and forty thousand fans, his biggest live audiences so far. In Japan, a country whose culture had remained close to Bowie's heart, he was treated like a returning hero and responded with a series of dazzling performances, the last of which took place at Tokyo's NHK Hall. The gig was filmed in its entirety and

Bowie on the set of *Saturday Night Live* in December 1979 with Klaus Nomi (left) and members of the cast, including (from top center) Bill Murray, Laraine Newman, Jane Curtin, and Gilda Radner.

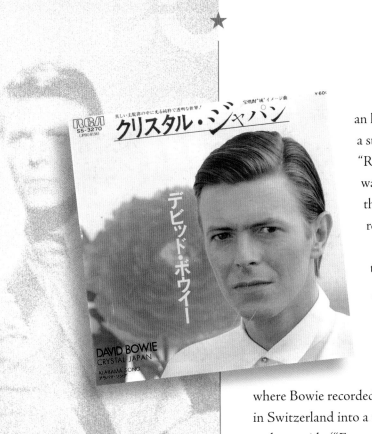

an hour-long edit was transmitted on Japanese television, providing a stunning document of the later version of the show, which omitted "Rock 'n' Roll Suicide" in favor of "Alabama Song." After the gig, there was a *Just a Gigolo*–themed party to celebrate the film's release early the next year. The group then flew home, but Bowie and Schwab remained in Tokyo to enjoy Christmas.

Bowie would not tour again for another four years, but the Isolar II world jaunt had enshrined his status as one of the greatest artists rock had ever seen and as a relentlessly creative individual who showed no sign of flagging. This impression of boundless inventiveness was further highlighted by the release of *Lodger* in May 1979. After a quiet start to the year, Bowie and Visconti had finished the album at New York's Power Plant, where Bowie recorded his vocals, transforming the experimental instrumentals recorded in Switzerland into a travelogue of songs concerning topics such as nuclear destruction and genocide ("Fantastic Voyage"), the ignoble art of playing other people's records ("D.J."), and the testosterone-fueled joys—and attendant sexual confusion—of young men coming of age ("Boys Keep Swinging"). Naturally, there were typically opaque moments too. Bowie amusingly admitted of "Red Sails," "I honestly don't know what it's about."

Lodger's sleeve featured a photograph taken by Brian Duffy of Bowie in a contorted pose reminiscent of an Egon Schiele portrait, with, as if he'd been the victim of an accident, his nose disturbingly flattened. The artwork didn't always endear itself to reviewers; nor did the music within, which was admittedly uneven though sporadically brilliant—as with "Fantastic Voyage," "Red Sails," "Look Back in Anger," and "Boys Keep Swinging." In the UK, it reached No. 4, though it fared less well in the States, peaking at No. 20. Both Bowie and Eno confessed a degree of disappointment with the record, and it would mark the end of their extraordinary fertile period of close collaboration. But the promo video for "Boys Keep Swinging," featuring Bowie camping it up gloriously in drag, would denote the start of a new creative relationship with director David Mallet, who would become crucial in the Bowie's development as a 1980s MTV icon.

Bridging the gap between *Lodger* and *Scary Monsters*, Bowie released two non-album singles in early 1980: the Japan-only "Crystal Japan" and a double-A-side pairing a version of Bertolt Brecht's "Alabama Song" with a stark reworking of Bowie's own "Space Oddity."

1980 – 1984
It's No Game

In January 1980, as a new decade dawned and Bowie turned thirty-three—the age when Christ supposedly met his maker—it was perhaps only natural that the singer should contemplate a fresh start. With the Berlin Trilogy wrapped up, his divorce from Angie in its final stages, and his fruitful working relationship with Brian Eno over—for now—it was a perfect time for a Bowie reboot. The 1970s had been the decade that propelled and defined the singer, taking him from playing a South London pub as a fading one-hit wonder to performing arena tours as one of rock's greatest and most beguiling stars. Yet three decades of extraordinary work were still to come.

Although 1979 was an unusually quiet year for Bowie, with no tour to promote *Lodger* and no other recording sessions of his own, it hadn't been without incident. Two of the most dramatic events concerned Lou Reed and Iggy Pop, the stars whose ailing careers he had revived by producing their early solo albums. In Iggy's case, Bowie had co-written his material, provided him with an income and a place to live, and performed in his touring band. But Bowie's largess could sometimes complicate these friendships, as an extraordinary episode in spring 1979 demonstrated. On April 10, Reed played at the Hammersmith Odeon to promote his album *The Bells* and during the set was unsettled to spot Bowie watching from the wings. Afterward, the two men went for dinner at the Chelsea Rendezvous restaurant, accompanied by their girlfriends and Lou's guitarist, Chuck Hammer. During the meal, Reed—whose recent albums had shown a dramatic decline in quality due to his continued substance abuse—was overheard asking Bowie if he'd produce his next record. Bowie responded, "Yes—if you clean up your act," to which an outraged Reed exploded, snarling, "Never say that to me!" and slapping his friend hard

(opposite)
Bowie conducts an interview with MTV at the Carlyle Hotel, New York, on January 27, 1983—the day his deal with EMI was announced.

across each cheek. The ex-Velvet was pulled away from Bowie and thrown out of the restaurant, leaving Bowie to stew over the attack. Later that night, Hammer heard Bowie thumping on the door of Reed's hotel room, hell-bent on seeking revenge, but his knock was never answered.

Bowie's friendships were put to the test yet again that summer, when he visited Iggy at Rockfield Studios in Wales, where he was recording *Soldier*, his second album for Arista. His first record for the label, *New Values*, had lacked the spontaneity and magic spark of the Bowie-produced *The Idiot* and *Lust for Life*, and, as with Reed, Iggy's career looked as if it was once more heading for the rocks. Bowie attended the sessions purely as Iggy's friend but perhaps inevitably became involved creatively, causing friction with the album's producer, Iggy's fellow ex-Stooge James Williamson, who quit the project. Steve New, formerly of Glen Matlock's post-Pistols group the Rich Kids, was drafted to play

(opposite)
Bowie with Keith Richards in the early 1980s. Bowie twice used Richards's Jamaica studio: in 1976 for rehearsals for the *Station to Station* tour and again in 1980 on the early stages of *Scary Monsters (and Super Creeps)*.

Bowie attends a press conference at the Keio Plaza Hotel, Tokyo, in April 1980.

guitar, but once again Bowie's presence caused ructions. According to Matlock, who played bass on the album, the flare-up involved New's girlfriend Patti Palladin. "Bowie was chatting up Patti because he believed she had a pack of cigarettes stashed in her room," Matlock told the author. "It was the middle of the night and everyone else had run out of them." New assumed Bowie was moving in on his girl and punched the singer; then, believing Iggy was mortified at his outburst, New declared he was pulling out of performing on Iggy's forthcoming US tour. This riled Iggy so much that he wiped the guitarist's contributions from the album, resulting in *Soldier*'s rather incomplete sound. "The ironic thing is that Iggy thought it was funny that Steve hit Bowie," added Matlock. "And also, even more ironic, Steve was the biggest Bowie fan I've ever met."

The start of Bowie's own new album was similarly dogged by misunderstandings when it came to guitar players. After Bowie's office engaged the services of Adrian Belew and reportedly paid him an advance, they never again contacted him. The trusted team of Carlos Alomar, George Murray, and Dennis Davis did, however, receive their now-customary invitations. Toward the end of 1979, Bowie and his aide Coco Schwab had rented an apartment on West 26th Street in Chelsea, and such was the singer's closeness to his rhythm guitarist that Alomar and his wife took a flat on the same block. Work began in February 1980 at Keith Richards's studio in Jamaica, used by Bowie four years earlier for the *Station to Station* tour rehearsals, and continued at the Power Station on West 53rd Street. This time, there was little sign of the experimental songwriting techniques that Bowie and Eno had employed on Bowie's previous three albums; instead the singer revisited discarded song ideas from the past, sketched out a few new ones on guitar, or directed the band with simple instructions.

According to Tony Visconti, in the producer's chair once more, there was a palpable sense, although it was never overtly expressed, that Bowie wanted to make a record with a mainstream commercial appeal that contrasted sharply with the cult, underground atmosphere of the Berlin-era albums. Clarity of purpose was helped by a fresh, forensic studio methodology. "Bowie walked in with a clipboard, he had a moustache, and was wearing a full-length leather coat with Japanese sandals, and a big wooden crucifix

(opposite)
Under Japanese influence: Bowie in Japanese-style overcoat circa 1979, and a picture-disc edition of "It's No Game," featuring a spoken-word vocal by Michi Hirota.

around his neck," Chuck Hammer told Bowie biographer Paul Trynka. "He was very open, but very organised."

A request to work up a tune around a Bo Diddley beat became the foundation of the soulful, church-y "Up the Hill Backwards," while the call for a "mid-paced groove" supplied the skeletal frame for "Fashion." "I Am a Laser," a song dating from the Astronettes session in 1973, was remade into what would become "Scream Like a Baby." Elsewhere, Bowie sketched out chord changes while the band filled in the gaps. Hammer, mischievously poached from Lou Reed after the Rendezvous scuffle, was asked to try out his new innovation, the synth-guitar, on the backing tracks for "Teenage Wildlife" and "Ashes to Ashes." Exploring a concept he'd devised called "guitarchitecture," involving the layering of synthesized guitar sounds, Hammer set to work. "It was very experimental even for us," recalled Visconti. "It was 50/50 if he would make the cut." Meanwhile, E-Street band pianist Roy Bittan, who was working elsewhere in the building on Springsteen's *The River*, provided the song's melancholic, minimalist keyboard motif. At Alomar's suggestion, the group also recorded a cover of "Kingdom Come," a recent solo song by Tom Verlaine, frontman and guitarist of New York art-rockers Television. Verlaine was asked to contribute guitar but, according to Visconti, spent so long fiddling around trying to find a decent sound on the numerous amplifiers he'd rented that his work was never used.

After a month's break, Bowie and Visconti relocated to the latter's Good Earth Studios in London's Soho, where Bowie planned to record his vocals and further collaborators were to join the fray. In an extraordinary return to his real-time composing technique on "Heroes," Robert Fripp created the jerky, metallic riff to "Fashion" in just a couple of takes, later explaining, "There's nothing you feel less like in the world than turning out a burning solo at 10:30 in the morning." Meanwhile, an ill-tempered Pete Townshend, fueled by Burgundy (and famously declaring, "There's no such thing as *white wine!*"), added guitar to "Because You're Young."

The album's lyrics, brewing in Bowie's mind since New York, were tackled last. One working title, "Is There Life After Marriage?," suggested Bowie's divorce from Angie was fresh in his mind—as would the final lyrics to "Up the Hill Backwards," with their reference to the possibilities offered by the "arrival of freedom." Among the most intriguing lyrics were those for "Ashes to Ashes," a curious essay in self-awareness that revives the

The iconic cover art for *Scary Monsters (and Super Creeps)* combined paintings by Edward Bell and photographs by longtime Bowie collaborator Brian Duffy.

Major Tom character from "Space Oddity" (endearingly referred to as from "such an early song"), and for "Teenage Wildlife," which poked fun at the "New Wave boys" of the New Romantic movement that, having been inspired to take up their synths by *Low*, "*Heroes*", and the *Stage* tour, were now threatening to steal Bowie's thunder. (The song's "broken-nosed mogul" was later identified by Gary Numan—in the public's mind a possible culprit himself—as Visage's Steve Strange.) Meanwhile, actress Michi Hirota, wife of musician Joji Hirota and one of the cover stars of Sparks' 1974 album *Kimono My House*, intoned a Japanese translation of the chilling lyrics for "It's No Game"—Bowie's reaction to the rise of far-right political parties in Britain—adding to the album's chic, avant-garde, catwalk feel.

For the sleeve artwork, Bowie called upon Edward Bell, an illustrator well known for his work in *Vogue* and *Tatler*, who was invited along to a photo session by *Aladdin Sane* cover photographer Brian Duffy, for which Bowie had dressed in his Pierrot costume. Bell took his own shots of the singer, taking off his makeup and outfit. "He had too much makeup on, but it looked good when it was smudged," Bell later recalled. "But what was so good was that he didn't just stand there. He saw the angle. Which was very much of its time: decadent glamour."

Bowie at the Blitz Club in London with Princess Julia in 1979, and the cover art to the following year's "Ashes to Ashes" single—the landmark promo video for which features several members of the Blitz scene.

Album and sleeve done, Bowie headed to New Romantic haven the Blitz club in Covent Garden, evolved from a weekly "Bowie Night," to cast extras—including Steve Strange—for the video for "Ashes to Ashes." The shoot was directed by David Mallet, who the previous year had filmed the camp promo for "Boys Keep Swinging." With a budget over $500,000, "Ashes to Ashes" was at the time the most expensive music video ever made and remains one of the most memorable. The scenes of the singer, dressed in his Pierrot costume designed by Natasha Korniloff and leading a parade of Blitz regulars like the head of a bizarre cult, proved an apt metaphor for *Scary Monsters'* impact. At a stroke, Bowie had reasserted himself as a beacon of modernity and as one of music's indefatigable visionaries. In September 1980, "Ashes to Ashes" hit No. 1 in the UK, with *Scary Monsters* soon after reaching the same position. In the States, the album made No. 12, his best showing since *Low*.

As with *Lodger*, Bowie showed no immediate interest in touring to support the album—the pressure to do so relieved by the international acclaim for the videos for "Ashes to Ashes" and "Fashion"—and by the time of its release had returned to his second love: acting. Film was never far from Bowie's orbit, and, indeed, while he was in London, he'd visited the set of *Breaking Glass* (named for his song) to watch Hazel O'Connor at work, the New Wave chanteuse having worked on the soundtrack with Visconti. This time, however, it wasn't a movie role that lured him but a part in a stage production of Bernard Pomerance's *The Elephant Man*. Bowie first saw the play in New York in December 1979 but thought no more of it until two months later when he was approached by its twenty-nine-year-old director, Jack Hofsiss, to star in a recast version of the show. Hofsiss had been greatly impressed by Bowie's performance in *The Man Who Fell to Earth* and sensed that the role of John Merrick, the grotesquely deformed character of the title who is rescued from a Victorian circus freak show by the surgeon Frederick Treves, shared much in common with Thomas Newton's misunderstood, persecuted alien. No formal offer was made to the singer until May, when Hofsiss gave Bowie just twenty-four hours to decide whether he would take the part, which entailed a month of rehearsals, preliminary appearances in Denver and Chicago, and a final three-month run that autumn at the Booth Theatre in New York. Exhilarated by the challenge of starring in a Broadway production and put on the spot, Bowie agreed and began his preparation by visiting the London Hospital, where Merrick's skeleton and personal effects were kept.

Although the national press was dissuaded from reviewing Bowie's debut as Merrick in Denver, the local notices were ecstatic. Bowie was keenly aware that a significant proportion of the audience was there to see him, rather than the play, which added to the pressure. "If I hadn't been successful in the first 15 or 20 minutes, then they'd have got up and started leaving, because it's not the kind of part you can fuck

(opposite)
Bowie onstage during a rehearsal for *The Elephant Man's* Broadway run, September 17, 1980.

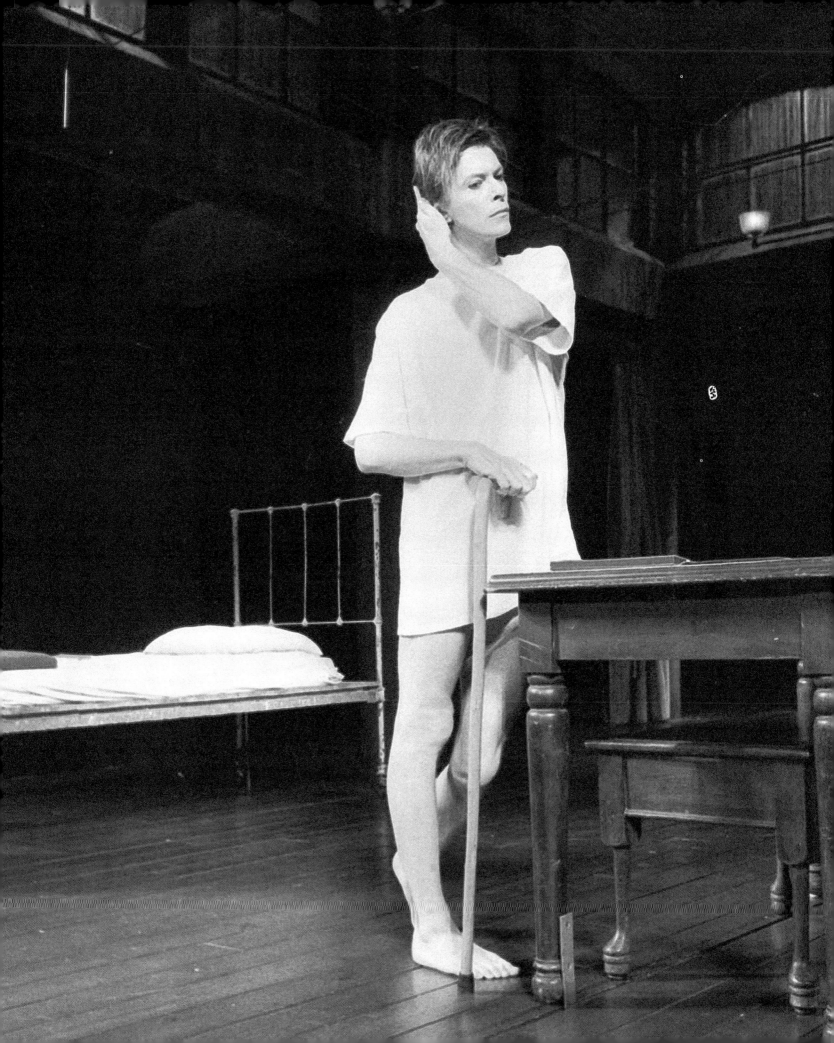

about with, frankly," he told *NME*'s Angus MacKinnon a few weeks later. "You've got to be credible." Bowie's raw talent as an actor was mercilessly tested as, unlike John Hurt in David Lynch's 1981 film version, who was hidden behind grotesque prosthetics, Bowie had to express the cruel eccentricities of Merrick's condition by contorting his face and body, initially clothed only in a loin cloth.

During the run in Chicago, it became apparent to the other players that their leading man was no ordinary jobbing actor. The crowds of fans waiting to see Bowie arrive at and leave the theater presented the producers with numerous security issues, and at one point the singer was obliged to travel to and from the venue in a garbage truck. His digs also had to be changed to a secret location, unknown even to the rest of the cast, whom he rewarded for their support and loyalty with generous weekly gifts. By the time *The Elephant Man* reached New York in September, Bowie had mastered the role, and the play became a box-office sensation. Bowie was not just selling millions of records but was now the toast of Broadway too. The opening night was attended by an impressive array of characters who'd observed his singular journey from cracked pop star to stage sensation, including Andy Warhol, Christopher Isherwood, Elizabeth Taylor, and Charlie Chaplin's widow, Oona. Also observing his triumphant Broadway debut were his mother and old manager Ken Pitt, both of whom he'd flown over from London.

Bowie was relishing life as a working stage actor and used his downtime in New York to renew his love affair with the city and catch up with old friends, including John Lennon and Yoko Ono, whom he'd last encountered at the nadir of his cocaine and amphetamine dependency. On December 8, 1980, after returning to his apartment after a performance, Bowie was stunned to learn that Lennon had been shot dead by Beatles fan Mark Chapman just a mile and a half away. Profoundly shaken and devastated at the loss of his friend, Bowie nevertheless refused an offer by Hofsiss to reduce his time on stage for the remaining performances, though security at the theater was significantly increased. It subsequently transpired that Chapman had seen *The Elephant Man* and photographed Bowie at the stage door, considering him a possible alternative target. Perhaps unsurprisingly, when the show completed its run in early January 1981, Bowie turned down the offer to continue in the role and left New York for his home in Switzerland, where he took a six-month break from work. He used the time to reconnect with Zowie (now known as Duncan) and hired an ex–Navy Seal to look after the family's security arrangements. Justifiably paranoid, he also moved several times, fearing for his safety. Plans to tour *Scary Monsters* in 1981 were shelved for good, denying fans the opportunity to see Bowie play live for a third consecutive year.

Bowie's return to the recording studio came, not for the last time in the 1980s, via an approach from a film production company rather than a record label. *Scary Monsters* had fulfilled the RCA contract that Tony Defries had brokered ten years earlier, closing

Bowie and co-star Nastassja Kinski at a screening of *Cat People*, April 1982.

one of the most fertile chapters in any artist-label relationship of the rock era (just one more new EP was to appear on the RCA imprint, the *Baal* EP). While Bowie was waiting for the term of the contract to expire, in early summer 1981, Paul Schrader, writer of *Taxi Driver* and director of *American Gigolo*, asked him to contribute vocals to the title song of his latest film, *Cat People*, whose score had been written by electro disco pioneer Giorgio Moroder. Bowie recorded his dark, smoldering vocal, arguably one of the finest of his career, at Mountain Studios, where he discovered Freddie Mercury and the rest of Queen hard at work on the album that would become *Hot Space*.

After adding a backing vocal part to the track "Cool Cat," which was never used, Bowie joined the group for a jam session that had transformed a Roger Taylor song called "Feel Like" into a new number, "Under Pressure." The catchy bassline was arrived at by accident. During dinner, John Deacon had forgotten what he'd played, and when

QUEEN & DAVID BOWIE
UNDER PRESSURE

The simple but effective cover art to Bowie's worldwide hit collaboration with Queen, "Under Pressure."

The *Baal* EP, for which Bowie returned to Berlin to record in September 1981. It would be his last collaboration with producer Tony Visconti for two decades.

Bowie reminded him by humming the riff, he added a different accent and note. The track was cooked up quickly, but while Bowie was accustomed to such spontaneous collaborations, Queen wasn't, and Brian May in particular wasn't overly impressed with the band accommodating such a strong outside influence. "I think 'Under Pressure' is one of the best things we ever did," Taylor told Mark Blake, author of the Queen biography *Is This the Real Life?*. "I got on well with David and so did Freddie. But five egos in the studio could be a bit much." Arguments continued over the mixing, which took place in New York without Bowie, but the result was deemed so powerful—and such a commercial no-brainer—that EMI pushed to release it as a single in October 1981, when it topped the UK chart, giving Bowie his third UK No. 1 and Queen its second.

Before the singer had cooked up "Under Pressure," he'd already committed to his next major project, which was the lead part in a BBC dramatization of German playwright Bertolt Brecht's first work, *Baal*. Written in 1918, Brecht's story centers around the life of a drunken, womanizing poet who leaves destruction and death in his wake without troubling his conscience—until it's too late. The director, Alan Clarke, had achieved notoriety two years earlier for *Scum*, the violent teenage prison drama, of which Bowie was a big admirer. Clarke and producer Louis Marks had flown to Switzerland to court the singer but were unaware until they met him of his vast knowledge of early twentieth-century German theater and art. The job entailed a month of rehearsals in West London, followed by a week-long shoot in August. Bowie signed up, and dressed in filthy rags with his teeth made to look rotten, he led the cast through the shoot with the utmost professionalism and dedication.

For authenticity's sake, Bowie wanted to record the music for *Baal* in Berlin, where he decamped in September with Visconti and the play's musical director, Dominic Muldowney. The lease of his apartment on Hauptstrasse had expired earlier in the year, so the three men booked into the Berlin Trilogy's storied bunkhouse, the Schlosshotel Gerhus. Working at the larger Hansa studio by the Wall, Bowie assembled a group that included a seventy-five-year-old musician who had worked with Brecht in the late 1920s, further adding to the

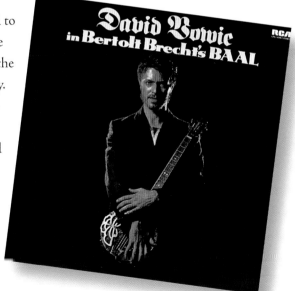

atmospheric charge of Muldowney's dark, disquieting arrangements. At night, Bowie gave Muldowney a guided tour of the city's sleazy underbelly of drag clubs and dive bars, as well as taking him to the Dschungel, the discotheque housed in the historic Femina-Palast ballroom dating from the 1920s. The EP of *Baal* material was released to coincide with the broadcast of play in March 1982, an event that perplexed some Bowie fans— especially those arriving in the wake of "Ashes to Ashes"—who were dismayed to see their dapper hero with decayed teeth, a beard, shabby clothes, a battered banjo, and few redeeming moral features. The critics, however, praised the singer's performance, though they were less complimentary about the play and production as a whole.

After completing the *Baal* EP, Bowie had begun a prolonged holiday and was occasionally spotted socializing in London nightspots. One evening, at the club Gossips, members of the Glaswegian punk band the Exploited were tickled when Bowie made a beeline for their table. "He recognised us and came over to talk," guitarist "Big" John Duncan told the author. "He wasn't being David Bowie, he was just this ordinary guy. He knew everything about us, he was a fan. I thought that was amazing! The only embarrassing thing was our bass player followed him about all night."

Bowie and costar Catherine Deneuve on the set of *The Hunger*.

JEREMY THOMAS PRODUCTION présente

UN FILM DE
NAGISA OSHIMA

FURYO

MERRY CHRISTMAS Mr LAWRENCE

DAVID BOWIE • TOM CONTI • RYUICHI SAKAMOTO • TAKESHI
JACK THOMPSON
Producteur associé JOYCE HERLIHY
producteurs exécutifs MASATO HARA • EIKO OSHIMA • GEOFFREY NETHERCOTT et TERRY CLINWOOD
musique RYUICHI SAKAMOTO
• scénario NAGISA OSHIMA avec PAUL MAYERSBERG d'après le roman de SIR LAURENS VAN DER POST
produit par JEREMY THOMAS • réalisé par NAGISA OSHIMA
filmé en [logo] DOLBY STEREO • COPYRIGHT NATIONAL FILM TRUSTEE COMPANY
distribué par AAA TOPFILMS

A film still and French promotional poster for *Merry Christmas, Mr. Lawrence* (known as *Furyo* in several European markets). The film was widely regarded as Bowie's best screen performance since *The Man Who Fell to Earth.*

Bowie's next ventures were, tellingly, film acting roles, further indication that he was still wary of returning to his music career after the trauma of Lennon's death. The first part was in *The Hunger*, a modern-day vampire movie directed by Tony Scott, starring Bowie and French film icon Catherine Deneuve as blood-thirsty, undead lovers. The voltage between the two principals didn't quite crackle as Scott had intended, however, and the film received lukewarm reviews. The second role was more intriguing and attracted far greater public interest. *Merry Christmas Mr. Lawrence* was based on Laurens van der Post's recollections of his incarceration in a World War II Japanese prisoner-of-war camp and was directed by Nagisa Oshima, whose *In the Realm of the Senses* had caused a sensation in 1976 for its real onscreen sex scenes and its denouement where the female lead severs her lover's penis and carries it around inside her.

Bowie couldn't pass up the opportunity to work with Oshima, and directly after *The Hunger* wrapped, he arranged to take a holiday in the South Pacific to be already in situ when filming began on the beautiful island of Rarotonga in September. Oshima was interested in using actors from outside the world of film, and having cast Bowie in the role of the tormented British officer Jack Celliers, he enlisted Yellow Magic Orchestra's

Chic's Nile Rodgers and Bernard Edwards in London in 1981, shortly before they collaborated with Bowie on *Let's Dance*.

Ryuichi Sakamoto as camp commandant Captain Yonoi and comedian Takeshi Kitano as Sergeant Hara. Meanwhile, veteran screen star Tom Conti took the role of van der Post's character, Lt. Col. John Lawrence. Bowie and Sakamoto proved to be judicious choices: the plot demanded an undercurrent of homoeroticism between the two officers, and the musician-actors, similarly androgynous and exotic, managed to convey the unspoken sexual tensions perfectly. Though not without moments of melodrama, Celliers was arguably Bowie's second-greatest screen performance after *The Man Who Fell to Earth* and brought him generous praise from the critics.

One evening while filming on Rarotonga, Bowie jammed a set of old R & B standards with Sakamoto (who would provide the movie's haunting score), an event that reflected Bowie's renewed interest in the music of his youth. Awaiting Oshima's arrival on the island, he had amused himself by playing homemade mixtapes featuring artists such as James Brown, Johnny Otis, Elmore James, Albert King, and other R & B favorites. What struck him was the simplicity, optimism, and purity of the music. After the film wrapped in October, he returned to New York, where he re-immersed himself in the city's music scene and hung out backstage with the Who and the Clash at their

Shea Stadium shows. It was around this time that he bumped into Chic's guitarist Nile Rodgers, who would become the key figure on his next album. There are various stories about how the pair met, but it was either in the bar at the Carlyle Hotel or at the Continental nightclub (with Billy Idol in attendance) that the two men fell into conversation, enthusing about their love of old R & B.

Rodgers, with bassist Bernard Edwards, had reshaped the sound of disco in the late 1970s with Chic's "Good Times" and "Le Freak," as well as with their production work with Sister Sledge and Diana Ross. But in the last year or so, Rodgers seemed to have lost his magic touch and was seeking a new way forward. It struck Bowie that Rodgers's clean, classic, dance-orientated production style might be combined with an old-fashioned R & B aesthetic to create a new kind of pop music—economical, slick, and punchy. The singer invited the guitarist to his new home in Lausanne, Switzerland, to sketch out some ideas for a new album. One song was called simply "Let's Dance," which Bowie performed to a bemused Rodgers on a twelve-string acoustic guitar with only six strings on it.

Rodgers later realized that during their Swiss sojourn, Bowie was quietly "programming" the guitarist, playing him records, such as the Isley Brothers'"Twist and Shout" and Duane Eddy's "Peter Gunn" theme, with a view to using elements of them on the new record. Bowie also played him Iggy Pop's "China Girl" from *The Idiot*, which the singer believed could be retooled into a huge dancefloor smash. He also wanted to have another stab at "Cat People (Putting Out Fire)"—a minor hit in its original form when it was released on MCA earlier that year to coincide with the film's release—and to cover the group Metro's 1977 Bowie-inspired synth-pop hit "Criminal World."

Sessions began at New York's Power Station in December 1982, with Rodgers pulling together a group including bassist Carmine Rojas and drummer Omar Hakim (whose father had played trumpet with Duke Ellington and Count Basie), as well as Chic's drummer Tony Thompson and keyboardist Rob Sabino. Rodgers's appointment as Bowie's co-producer meant that Visconti, whom Bowie had originally asked to make the record, was left out in the cold; so too were Carlos Alomar, who turned down what he considered an "embarrassing" fee to perform on the album, George Murray, and Dennis Davis. The insulting offer may have been Bowie's way of letting Alomar down gently, as for several months, he'd had another guitarist in mind for the job, a twenty-eight-year-old Texan named Stevie Ray Vaughan, whose group Double Trouble had wowed the Montreux Jazz Festival earlier in the year, with Bowie looking on from the wings. Vaughan's natural style was tough blues rock, which Bowie felt could add a piquant flavor to his re-imagined, modern R & B sound. "Stevie was fantastic," Rodgers told Bowie biographer David Buckley, author of *Strange Fascination*. "That is why I believe David Bowie is an absolute genius, because he was able to see the great fusion of styles between my background, his background and Stevie Ray. David had a feeling, a premonition, that this would work."

The album was completed within three weeks, unusually without Bowie contributing any instrumental parts, Rodgers manning the mixing console while Bowie directed proceedings from the sofa in the control room. The sessions adhered to civilized hours—from 10:30 a.m. to 6:00 p.m.—and had little of the willful experimentation heard on Bowie's previous albums. His role this time was as "The Singer," placing his voice and persona center stage, just as the star vocalists did in the days of the R & B big bands. Most of his performances, captured in the last two days of recording, were first takes, while the lyrical content of his new songs was simple and positive (in stark contrast to the moody, sexually ambivalent subject matter of the cover of "Criminal World").

The cover art to *Let's Dance*, the most commercially successful album of Bowie's career.

Bowie used the tapes to try to close a new record deal with EMI, which together with the other main label was naturally eager to sign him. RCA wanted to renegotiate its terms with the singer, but after the travails of the MainMan years and its unenthusiastic reaction to *Low* (which Bowie *still* smarted about), it had further offended him in the run-up to Christmas by releasing a single of his and Bing Crosby's "Peace on Earth/Little Drummer Boy," a recording Bowie detested. On January 27, 1983, Bowie finally inked a contract with EMI worth a reported $17 million, a vast sum which would bankroll his studio work until the end of the decade.

Two years after Lennon's death, it was evident that Bowie was now ready to re-enter the pop world and play live again. After making a cameo in the comedy pirate romp *Yellowbeard* while on holiday in Mexico, he offered an olive branch to Alomar, hiring the guitarist as musical director for the *Serious Moonlight* world tour, an ambitious jaunt that by the end of 1983 would notch up almost a hundred performances in sixteen different countries, with ticket sales topping the $2.5 million mark. While Alomar recruited what was essentially the *Let's Dance* studio group, Bowie traveled to Australia with David Mallet to shoot videos for the first two singles from the album, the title track and "China Girl."

The promo film for "Let's Dance," where a sun-bleached Bowie performs the song in the bar of the remote Carinda Hotel in the outback of New South Wales while two young Aboriginals, Joelene King and Terry Roberts, dance to the music, is one of the most memorable of the 1980s. The 2015 documentary, *Let's Dance: Bowie Down Under*, revealed that the nugget-y-faced locals weren't forewarned of King's and Roberts's roles so that their reactions—mostly perplexed/disapproving glances—were spontaneous. Bowie referred to the promo as "a very direct statement about integration of one culture

"with another"—something that also rang true of the "China Girl" shoot, which saw Bowie rolling around in the surf on a beach, *From Here to Eternity*–style, with New Zealand actress Geeling Ng. "Can I point out, contrary to popular belief, David and I did not have sex on the beach," Ng told *Q* magazine in 2009. "It was shot at 5 a.m., the water was freezing and wasn't a great lubricant, and we were being watched by a film crew and joggers passing by. Not very romantic." The shoot did, however, mark the beginning of a short relationship between Bowie and Ng.

The release of "Let's Dance" as a single in March 1983 signaled the beginning of a new phase in Bowie's career, when the international fame of his RCA years was eclipsed by superstar status. Part of this was due to the launch in 1981 of MTV, the cable channel devoted to broadcasting music videos. Though MTV's influence on record sales in the very early 1980s has been overstated—it wasn't until 1983 that it became widely available to subscribers in some of the United States' biggest cities, and in Europe the format didn't take off until the 1990s—it proved to be the perfect vehicle for promoting Bowie, an artist who'd been making memorable promo videos since the *Aladdin Sane* days. Bowie was naturally supportive of a channel that played music 24/7, but during an MTV interview to promote *Let's Dance*, he joined the chorus of musicians

A Japanese edition of "China Girl," the second single from *Let's Dance*, and a song Bowie originally co-wrote with Iggy Pop for *The Idiot*.

An advertisement for Bowie's *Serious Moonlight* tour—his first world tour since 1978.

enraged that few videos featuring black artists were never aired, a policy mercifully reversed in subsequent years.

By the time Bowie joined the tour rehearsals in April, "Let's Dance" was No. 1 on both sides of the Atlantic, with the album soon to follow suit. The touring band was his biggest yet, and as well as Carlos Alomar, Tony Thompson, Carmine Rojas, and keyboardist David Lebolt, it included a three-man saxophone section—dubbed the Borneo Horns—plus brothers Frank and George Simms on backing vocals. The lead

guitarist's job initially fell to Stevie Ray Vaughan, but toward the end of rehearsals in Dallas, Vaughan's hometown, a number of incidents set him on a collision course with Bowie and his management. The first was the sequence in the video for "Let's Dance" where Bowie mimed to the guitarist's solo, a seemingly innocent act which nonetheless outraged the purist, authenticity-obsessed Vaughan. The second was the realization that Vaughan's group, Double Trouble, would not be the support act during certain legs of the tour, as he had apparently been led to believe. The third was money—his manager was, at the last minute, angling for a higher fee for his client. It was also reported that the hard-living Vaughan was incredulous that the group's contracts demanded they steer clear of drugs, an activity Bowie had once so freely enjoyed. With the tour bus set to leave for the airport, from whence the group was due to fly to Europe, Bowie's team called Vaughan's bluff over his demands for a bigger wage and his other gripes and left him on the pavement with his gear. "One of the most heart-breaking things I've ever seen," recalled an emotional Rojas. (Vaughan would, however, go on to achieve international fame before tragically dying in a helicopter crash in 1990.)

With just days before the first show in Brussels, Bowie called Earl Slick, whom he had last encountered on the *Station to Station* sessions before they had fallen out amid the chaos of MainMan's dismissal. Over dinner in Paris, Bowie and Slick settled their differences, and after four days locked in Alomar's hotel room learning the act, the guitarist joined the group for the opening night of the tour at the eight-thousand-

Another shot of Bowie on the *Let's Dance* tour, flanked by keyboard player Dave Lebolt and sax men Steve Elson, Stan Harrison, and Lenny Pickett. His band for the tour also featured longtime collaborators Carlos Alomar and Earl Slick on guitar.

The final *Let's Dance* single, "Without You," with cover art by the American artist and activist Keith Haring.

The *Serious Moonlight* concert film was recorded at the Pacific Coliseum in Vancouver, Canada, on September 12, 1983, and released on VHS and laserdisc the following year.

capacity Vorst Nationaal arena in Brussels. For the stage set, as with the *Station to Station* and *Stage* tours, Bowie opted for simplicity and for drama relied on powerful and imaginative lighting effects devised by Mark Ravitz, who'd overseen the most extravagant leg of the *Diamond Dogs* tour. The daily regimen emphasized Bowie's interest in keeping fit, with morning aerobics sessions and healthy meals. His image for the tour was an updated 1950s rock 'n' roll look, with a bleach-blond quiff and a series of striking pastel-colored suits designed by Peter Hall. Meanwhile, the group was dressed in theatrical costumes—Alomar as a prince, Rojas as a Far Eastern sailor, the Simms brothers in boating garb, and Earl Slick, to his relief, as his unalloyed rock 'n' roll self. The setlist was as diverse as the costumes and revisited material from all of Bowie's 1970s albums, bar *The Man Who Sold the World*, with new arrangements that kept the Borneo Horns busy—and Bowie too, who on various numbers played guitar and sax.

As well as the arena dates, there were also several summer festival engagements, including the vast Us Fest in San Bernardino, for which Bowie was paid a fee of $1.5 million, spent on building a second stage set that would allow the crews to leapfrog ahead

to next dates. At Milton Keynes Bowl in the UK and Madison Square Garden, a large globe, lit to glow like a moon, was suspended high above the crowd, disgorging balloons at the show's finale. At Hammersmith Odeon, which served as a warmup for the outdoor Milton Keynes shows, Bowie called in Tony Visconti to sort out problems with the sound— which he did, while declining the offer of soundman for the rest of the tour. It would be another fifteen years before he and Bowie worked together again.

The North American leg of the tour ran from mid-July through mid-September and, with his fear of flying long conquered, Bowie traveled when necessary on his own specially chartered jet. In

Released in 1984, *Tonight* featured only two new Bowie originals. The rest of its nine tracks comprised cover versions and re-recordings of songs he had previously cut with Iggy Pop.

Vancouver, on September 3, he was unexpectedly reacquainted with Mick Ronson, who was in town working with a band. Ronson had requested guest tickets for the show from Coco Schwab and met Bowie backstage afterward. Bowie, who hadn't spoken to his *Ziggy* sidekick since 1975, invited him to join the group on stage the following evening for an encore of "The Jean Genie," which he duly thrashed his way through on a guitar borrowed from Earl Slick. In October, the tour moved on to Japan, then to Australia and New Zealand. On the final night of the tour, at Auckland's Western Springs Stadium on November 26, Bowie performed to a crowd of almost seventy-five thousand, at that point deemed to be the biggest-ever public gathering in New Zealand's history.

After the tour ended, Bowie elected to stay in the Far East, and in December several further dates were appended to the scheduled, using a stripped-down version of the stage set. His visits to Singapore, Bangkok, and Hong Kong were documented in *Ricochet*, a fascinating hour-long film by director Gerry Troyna, comprising fly-on-the-wall footage and staged scenes. "I came over to Japan in '72 [sic], I think it was, and I've had an ongoing affair with the East ever since," Bowie explained at a press conference in Hong Kong. The film provides an interesting counterpoint to David Mallet's official document of the tour, *Serious Moonlight*, a solid performance video that, in its original VHS form, including interview segments.

The tour ended on a poignant note. The last night in Hong Kong, on December 8, marked the third anniversary of John Lennon's murder. To commemorate his passing, Earl Slick, who'd worked on Lennon and Ono's *Double Fantasy* album, suggested the group play "Across the Universe" as recorded by Bowie for *Young Americans*. The singer countered with the idea of performing "Imagine," which the band duly did to a predictably emotional response. Tour over, Bowie and Schwab stayed on to holiday in the Far East with Iggy and his girlfriend Suchi Asano, visiting Bali and Java. Having relapsed throughout the early 1980s and believing he was the subject of a voodoo curse, Iggy was now in recovery, and as Bowie had revealed at the Hong Kong press conference, he was in the game for producing Iggy's next album.

The *Serious Moonlight* tour had been spectacular, and there was no doubt that, as 1984 dawned, Bowie was one of the biggest acts on the planet, occupying the

(opposite)
Bowie and Tina Turner duet on "Tonight" at the NEC in Birmingham, England, March 23, 1985.

same elevated tier of multimillion-selling artists as Michael Jackson, the Police, and Lionel Ritchie. *Let's Dance* had racked up sales of six million copies, boosting Bowie's back catalog along the way. But being a megastar wasn't a status Bowie necessarily felt comfortable with. In acquiring mainstream appeal, he sensed that he'd become disconnected from his real fans: "I suddenly didn't know my audience and, worse, I didn't care about them," he later admitted. But having delivered EMI with one blockbuster, the pressure was on to provide another, and by May 1984, he was back in the studio working on the follow-up to *Let's Dance*.

Perhaps it was inevitable that after twenty years and fifteen studio albums, Bowie's extraordinary creative élan would begin to wither. When recording began at Le Studio near Montreal, his desire to create another landmark record appears to have evaporated. The location had been chosen by Hugh Padgham, the Police's producer, with whom Bowie wanted to work—though it was agreed that Padgham would concede overall control to Derek Bramble, a former member of the Brit-funk group Heatwave. Bowie had been impressed by demos Bramble had produced for Brit soul singer Jaki Graham and was also intrigued at the idea of the Anglo-Caribbean Londoner providing an authentic reggae feel to the record.

But as soon as work on the record began—with Alomar, Rojas, and Hakim, plus the Borneo Horns, recalled for duty—Bowie appeared much more enthusiastically "bored." Though Bowie's vision for the album seemed to favor blending white reggae and soft blue-eyed soul, the two new originals he was keen to record, "Loving the Alien" and "Blue Jean," didn't necessarily suit either of those styles. A *raison d'être* for the album, if not any unifying musical style, was finally settled on by the arrival of Iggy Pop. Perhaps with the success of the remade "China Girl" in mind, Bowie now envisioned *Tonight*, as it would be titled, as another classic Bowie/Iggy collaboration. Instead of producing Iggy's new album, they would work on Bowie's album together.

Together, the two artists debated which songs from their past adventures could be resuscitated. In the end, they chose "Tonight" from *Lust for Life*, which was denuded of its original reference to a heroin overdose and given to guest vocalist Tina Turner to sing, and "Don't Look Down" from Iggy's *New Values*, which as with the title track was given an insipid pop-reggae makeover. "Neighborhood Threat," also from *Lust to Life*, was revisited too, while Bowie and Iggy together penned two brand-new songs, "Tumble and Twirl" and "Dancing with the Big Boys," the latter also credited to Alomar. The inclusion of covers of the Beach Boys' "God Only Knows" and Chuck Jackson's "I Keep Forgettin'" were subsequently justified by Bowie as an attempt to add a *Pin-Ups*-style dimension to the record, paying homage to songs that had touched him as a young man. But neither did its original much justice.

In subsequent years, Bowie would lament the fact that *Tonight* wasn't realized as powerfully as it could have been and was particularly disappointed with the released version of "Loving the Alien," which he'd originally recorded by himself in Montreux. "You should hear [it] on demo," he told *Q's* Adrian Deevoy in 1989. "It's a *wonderful* demo, I promise you! What am I meant to say?" Yet "Loving the Alien" and "Blue Jean" would sit seamlessly within his illustrious canon and showed that, left to his own devices, Bowie still had a knack for writing unusual and magnificent hit material.

On September 21, 1984, a full-length promo film for "Blue Jean" was premiered on UK TV amid a crackle of expectancy. Made by Sex Pistols filmmaker Julien Temple and twenty-one minutes long, it saw the singer in the dual roles of window cleaner Vic and an exotic Far East pop star Screaming Lord Byron. At the denouement, Byron steals Vic's date, to which the window cleaner froths, "You conniving, randy, bogus-Oriental old queen! Your record sleeves are better than your songs!" The real-life Bowie was having fun at his own expense, of course, but some critics felt that Vic may have had a point. "Blue Jean" and the subsequent singles "Tonight" and "Loving the Alien" sold well, and *Tonight* topped the chart in the UK and made No. 11 in the States, but reviews of what Bowie described as his "attempt to keep hold of my new audience" were decidedly mixed.

The singer's career would begin to plateau over the next decade or so, but until his renaissance in the three years before his death, he would never lose his ability to surprise and innovate—and no more so evident than in his decision to forsake pop music entirely and become the singer in a hard-rock outfit called Tin Machine.

CHAPTER 8

1985 – 2016
Little Wonder

A t 7:23 p.m. UK time on July 13, 1985, David Bowie took the stage at Wembley Stadium to perform for an audience of seventy-two thousand, plus an estimated worldwide television audience of nearly two billion. The occasion was Live Aid, the fundraising event for famine-hit Ethiopia, organized by the Boomtown Rats' singer Bob Geldof. Bowie's presence on the bill was no surprise—after the huge sales of *Let's Dance* and *Tonight*, and as an icon of the MTV generation, he was now one of the biggest mainstream artists on the planet. But few in the vast crowd watching his short set, ending with a passionate rendition of "Heroes," were aware that the concert represented Bowie's return to the public eye after a difficult six months of reflection, and that, far from being meticulously rehearsed, his hastily assembled group had only run through their set three times.

The year had begun with the release of the majestic "This Is Not America," a song Bowie had written and recorded with the Pat Metheny Group for the spy movie *The Falcon and the Snowman*. But in London, a tragic family drama was unfolding involving Bowie's half-brother Terry Burns. On January 16, Burns walked out of Cane Hill hospital, where he was still undergoing treatment for mental health issues, placed his body across a nearby railway line, and awaited his fate. His death shocked Bowie's family and prompted the singer's aunt Pat to complain to the tabloids about Bowie's alleged neglect of his brother over the previous decade or so. The public airing of such a private family matter deeply affected the singer, and he retreated to his home in Switzerland. In April, when Julien Temple arrived in Lausanne to shoot a video for "Loving the Alien," Bowie explained that he didn't feel able to participate. He apologized but stressed that he remained committed to appearing in Temple's feature film version of Colin MacInnes's 1959 novel *Absolute Beginners*, which was due to shoot in July. He also confirmed that he would fulfill his promise to record some songs for the soundtrack.

(opposite)
Bowie gives his final live performance, singing "Life on Mars!" at a *Keep a Child Alive* benefit in New York City, November 9, 2006.

Bowie confers with Roger Taylor and Brian May of Queen at the Live Aid concert at Wembley Stadium, London, July 13, 1985. In the front row, organizer Bob Geldof discusses the performances with Prince Charles. Later, Bowie's four-song set list not surprisingly included "Heroes".

Bowie had been interested in Temple's film ever since the idea had been suggested several years before. The story of *Absolute Beginners* had strong elements of autobiography for the singer, from its hip protagonist coming of age in late-1950s, jazz-obsessed London to the birth of the teenager and the rise of consumerism. Bowie had been cast in the film as sleazy advertising executive Vendice Partners, whose main scene involved him dancing on a giant typewriter to a song titled "That's Motivation." Feeling revitalized, Bowie booked into Abbey Road Studios in June to record the number, with session musicians including former Prefab Sprout guitarist Kevin Armstrong, ex–Soft Boys bassist Matthew Seligman, and the Attractions' keyboardist Steve Nieve. At the end of the session, Bowie unveiled a rough idea he had for the film's main theme tune. As it wasn't complete, "Absolute Beginners" was laid down that evening in sections, as it was written, with none of the musicians quite knowing where the song was going next. The result was one of Bowie's finest compositions of the 1980s, a stirring, happy-sad reflection on teenage romance that would reach No. 2 in the UK when it was released as a single the following year.

It was during the Abbey Road session that Bowie dropped a bombshell on the group—Mick Jagger would be joining them to record a version of

Martha and the Vandellas' "Dancing in the Street" to accompany a video that would be screened during the Live Aid concert. The original idea was that Bowie and Jagger would perform a live transatlantic duet via a satellite link, but it was decided that the time delay would make this impossible. Instead, Jagger, Bowie, and the group gathered at producer Alan Winstanley's West Side studios in Holland Park and taped the track in four hours. Job done, director David Mallet then whisked Bowie and Jagger away to London's then-derelict Docklands to shoot the hilarious promo film, in which the two old friends try to out-camp each other with ridiculous imitations of the other's stage moves.

Bowie's appearance two weeks later at Wembley Stadium, in a slot sandwiched between Queen and the Who, was triumphant, even though the group—essentially the *Absolute Beginners* session players—had little time to prepare the set, ultimately cut short

so a film reminding viewers of the terrible famine conditions in East Africa could be shown. Such was the enthusiastic reaction to the good-natured frolicking of the "Dancing in the Street" video, screened twice during the day, that the track was eventually released at the end of the summer, gifting Bowie with yet another UK No. 1.

After *Absolute Beginners* wrapped in August, Bowie began work on another film, the children's fantasy drama *Labyrinth*. The movie, written by Monty Python's

Bowie cut three very different non-album singles 1985: the Pat Metheny Group collaboration "This Is Not America," the epic ballad "Absolute Beginners," and a duet with Mick Jagger on "Dancing in the Street," released to raise money for famine relief.

Terry Jones and directed by Muppets creator Jim Henson, told the story of a teenage girl, Sarah, who fancifully wishes that goblins would steal away her younger brother. Jareth, the Goblin King—played by Bowie—obliges, and a contrite Sarah embarks on a fantastical quest to rescue her sibling, with Jareth breaking into song on the numbers Bowie contributed to the soundtrack. Shooting done, the singer then took an extended break with Iggy and Suchi in Mustique, where he'd brought a property, before returning with the couple to Switzerland for a skiing holiday in Gstaad. "I enjoy [skiing] and knew Jim—Iggy—would too, because Jim is incredibly athletic," he explained to *Smash Hits'* Tom Hibbert. "I taught him to ski. He's a very good skier."

Iggy remained with Bowie in Switzerland to record his next solo album, *Blah-Blah-Blah*, with Bowie co-producing with Mountain Studios house engineer David Richards. The record included several Bowie co-writes, including the title track and the wonderful "Shades," together with three collaborations with the Sex Pistols' Steve Jones and a cover of Johnny O'Keefe's vintage rocker "Real Wild Child." These

(opposite)
Bowie's best-known film role was the musical fantasy *Labyrinth*, in which he starred as Jareth, the Goblin King.

Bowie and Iggy Pop at the Ritz in New York City, 1986.

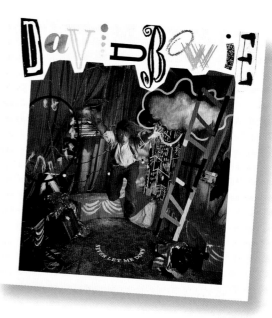

Though its name might suggest otherwise, *Never Let Me Down*, released in 1987, is widely considered to be Bowie's worst solo album.

Tickets to a pair of *Glass Spider* dates at Wembley Stadium, London, in June 1987. Bowie played to around 140,000 fans across the two shows.

sessions reunited Bowie with multi-instrumentalist Erdal Kizilçay, with whom Bowie had written the title theme for *When the Wind Blows*, the animated film of Raymond Briggs's harrowing anti-nuclear war story. In October, the singer and Kizilçay started to sketch out the songs for Bowie's next album, *Never Let Me Down*, with the addition of Carmine Rojas, Carlos Alomar, and Bowie's old school friend Peter Frampton on lead guitar. The sessions were completed at New York's Power Station studios, where Bowie wrote and recorded the title track, inspired by Coco Schwab's unflinching loyalty as his personal assistant, in a single day. The record was, however, over polished and uncharacteristically short on highlights—though it did have its moments, including the propulsive "Beat of Your Drum" and stirring "Zeroes," as well as the amusing mid-song rap on "Shining Star (Makin' My Love)" by the actor Mickey Rourke, whom Bowie had befriended that year in London. In later years, Bowie would distance himself from the record, describing it as an "awful album" and admitting "I didn't really apply myself." Visconti, estranged from the singer after contributing a candid interview to Peter and Leni Gillman's unforgiving 1986 biography *Alias David Bowie*, concurred that at this time "[David] let other people do his work," a development he found "tragic."

(opposite)
Bowie onstage at the Feijenoord Stadium in Rotterdam during his extravagant *Glass Spider* tour, May 29, 1987.

The *Glass Spider* world tour that followed in 1987 to promote the album met with the same critical derision meted out to *Never Let Me Down*, with the press corps deeply unimpressed by the huge mechanical arachnid that dominated the stage set and the extravagant convulsions of a five-piece dance troupe directed by the *Diamond Dogs* tour choreographer—and by now pop star in her own right—Toni Basil. The core of the group assembled for the occasion included Alomar, Rojas, Frampton, and drummer Alan Childs, but for many who witnessed the shows, the music seemed to play second fiddle to the opulent staging and theatrics. On the European leg, only an emotional performance at Berlin's Platz der Republik on June 6, 1987, when thousands of East German fans gathered on the far side of the Wall and sang along to "Heroes," matched the levels of emotional intensity for which Bowie gigs were renowned. Two years later, Bowie attributed the lackluster ambience to the crushing level of detail he was compelled to deal with on a daily basis. "There was too much responsibility on the last tour," he told *Q* magazine in 1989. "I was under stress every day. It was so big and unwieldly and everybody had a problem all the time, and I was under so much pressure. It was unbelievable." When the tour wound up in New Zealand at the end of November, Bowie and the crew vented their frustrations by symbolically torching the giant spider in a field near the venue. "That was such a relief!" he explained.

Bowie's reaction to becoming what he described as a "well-accepted artist," something he "never wanted to be," was to submerge himself in a project designed to be defiantly anti-mainstream and restore his credibility as rock's coolest maverick. Having turned forty at the start of 1987, Bowie concluded that, rather than softening his sound further, it was high time he rediscovered hard rock. The catalyst was his friendship with Reeves Gabrels, the husband of Sara Terry, his PR during the US leg of the *Glass Spider* tour. "I never told [David] I was a musician, because I didn't want to appear an opportunist," Gabrels told writer Martin O'Gorman. "He thought I was a painter because we used to talk about fine art, or anything except music. One time we were watching *Fantasy Island* backstage with the sound down, making up the plot ourselves." When Bowie discovered Gabrels was a composer and multi-instrumentalist, he invited him to work on a new version of *Lodger*'s "Look Back in Anger" to accompany a performance by dance troupe La La La Human Steps at London's Dominion Theatre, as part of a fundraising event for the Institute of Contemporary Arts. Soon afterward, the singer had the idea of forming a rock band with Gabrels on guitar and his old friends Tony and Hunt Sales, Iggy's rhythm section on *Lust for Life* and *The Idiot* tour.

The first rehearsals for what would become Tin Machine took place at the casino in Montreux in July 1988, where the group vibed themselves up by listening to live bootlegs of Cream, Led Zeppelin, and Jimi Hendrix. The guiding principle, it was explained, was to make as unholy a racket as possible. Bowie and Gabrels would

communicate their musical ideas through references to art and architecture. Tension between the devoutly cerebral Gabrels and the more streetwise Sales brothers—whose father Soupy would perform routines over the phone to the band, to much hilarity—created a powerful sound that *Rolling Stone*'s David Fricke later exquisitely described as "Sonic Youth meets *Station to Station*." For Bowie, the experience was exhilarating but also unnerving. "It was throwing myself into a group format, which is something I hadn't done . . . forever, really," he explained. "To have other members of the band making decisions was difficult."

The self-titled debut album by Bowie's divisive new group, Tin Machine.

The group began work on a Tin Machine album at Mountain Studios before upping sticks to Compass Point in Nassau, by that time guitarist Kevin Armstrong had joined them as an unofficial fifth member. The presence of Bowie's new girlfriend Melissa Hurley, a dancer on the *Glass Spider* tour, inspired the confessional "Prisoner of Love," while a visit from Sean Lennon prompted a cover of his father's "Working Class Hero." Elsewhere, Bowie's impulse to fashion a new strain of gritty, challenging art-rock resulted in the coruscating social commentary of "Crack City" and "I Can't Read," with its approving nod toward Joy Division's icy post-punk. (Joy Division had started life as

Tin Machine—Reeves Gabrels, Tony Sales, Hunt Sales, and Bowie—at the Paradiso, Amsterdam, June 24, 1989.

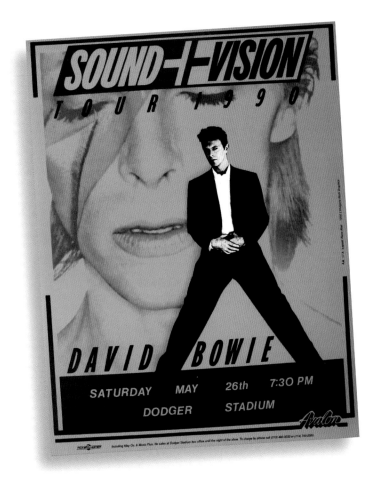

A poster for Bowie's *Sound + Vision* tour, which at the time he claimed would be the last chance for fans to hear his greatest hits onstage.

Warsaw, of course, after Bowie's "Warszawa.") The group made its debut at a local bar in Nassau, in front of a stunned audience of holidaymakers wondering why on earth Live Aid star David Bowie was fronting an experimental hard-rock band.

The group's debut album, *Tin Machine*, was released in May 1989, and the group embarked on a series of club dates. The interest in Bowie's new project was intense, though the initial sales of around two hundred thousand copies were modest compared with Bowie's previous three EMI albums. As a repositioning exercise, the album achieved everything it set out to do, and though the music wasn't to everyone's taste, the singer's courageous left turn signaled the end of a checkered, mainstream late 1980s. But with Bowie's new spirit of adventure came a desire to remind the world of his extraordinary legacy, which he now negotiated to become available to a new generation of fans via Rykodisc's superlative CD reissues of his RCA back catalog.

Plans for a world tour in 1990, taking the form of a straightforward greatest hits set, meant that sessions for a second Tin Machine album were interrupted. Instead, for the *Sound + Vision* dates, named for a retrospective career box set of the same name, Bowie recruited a new, stripped-down group, featuring Erdal Kizilçay on bass, guitarist Adrian Belew—who since the Stage tour and *Lodger* had become a mainstay in King Crimson—plus two members from Belew's solo band, keyboardist Rick Fox

and drummer Michael Hodges. Reeves Gabrels had been approached to play guitar but declined on the grounds that it would undermine the integrity of Tin Machine. The scale of the outing was impressive even by the standards set by the *Serious Moonlight* and *Glass Spider* tours, with 108 shows in twenty-seven countries. To signal the inclusive nature of the gigs—widely regarded as some of Bowie's most entertaining ever—fans were invited to vote for their favorite songs in a telephone poll, which would be reflected in the final setlist. It was also declared, somewhat prematurely, that the tour was to be the last ever to feature Bowie's old hits. Naturally, demand for tickets was overwhelming, and by the time the tour finished at Buenos Aires' River Plate Stadium on September 29, 1990, the box office receipts had topped an estimated $20 million.

It was in Buenos Aires that Bowie experienced a romantic epiphany that would change his life forever—he met his future wife Iman, the Somali-born but United States–based supermodel. Belew recalled Bowie stopping at her photograph while flicking through a fashion magazine on a flight between shows and announcing he wanted to date her. "I think lightning struck," the guitarist told David Buckley. "Just looking at her picture, he got interested in her." Later, he revealed that he was nervous that his sense of humor and enthusiasm for bad jokes would put her off—it didn't, and in 1992 they married in Switzerland.

With the *Sound + Vision* tour proving an uproarious success, Bowie returned to making *Tin Machine II*, which was released in September 1991 and promoted with a seventy-date world tour of medium-sized theaters that began in Dublin two weeks after the record appeared and ended at Tokyo's hallowed Budokan Hall in April 1992. The album was more extreme and abrasive than the band's debut, with Gabrels citing the industrial rock of Nine Inch Nails as a strong influence, and "Shopping for

Bowie and his soon-to-be wife Iman, in New York City in the summer of 1990, during a break between *Sound + Vision* shows.

Girls" and "You Can't Talk" remain overlooked pearls. For some fans, however, the group's onstage sonic firefights were too challenging, and at several venues, the audiences thinned out dramatically towards the end of the show. Backstage, the atmosphere was no less tense. "The split was [ultimately] down to the simple fact that the band had four radically different personalities rubbing up against each other to the point of great irritation," recalled Gabrels. Hunt Sales's predilection for rock 'n' roll excess was one difficult issue the band faced; another was the thorny issue of finance, as Bowie was underwriting the venture and reportedly losing money. Five years earlier, Bowie had been a critically immolated for being a mega-earning, airbrushed stadium superstar; now he was a misunderstood cult artist with his accountants on his back.

Tin Machine's second and final studio album, *Tin Machine II*.

Bowie would later claim that Tin Machine "charged me up—I can't tell you how much," at a time when he'd been artistically adrift. But his next album, 1993's *Black Tie White Noise*, was evidently a bid to reclaim the mainstream audience he had so successfully courted in the 1980s. His abiding connection with ordinary music fans, many of whom probably regarded Tin Machine as a bizarre blip in his career, was demonstrated soon after that band's final dates in Japan. On April 20, Bowie performed at a tribute concert at Wembley Stadium for Freddie Mercury, who had died of an AIDS-related illness in November 1991. Fronting a group built around the surviving members of Queen, Bowie performed "Under Pressure" with Annie Lennox. Mott the Hoople's Ian Hunter and Mick Ronson—at this stage terminally ill with liver cancer—joined him for "All the Young Dudes," with Bowie playing sax, and then, after Hunter departed, they played an emotional rendering of "Heroes." At the end of the song, Bowie dropped dramatically to his knees and recited the Lord's Prayer, dedicating it to a playwright friend in New York ill with AIDS. The recital was unscripted, and Bowie later admitted that, such was the spontaneity of the act that "the most surprised person there was me."

Bowie's first solo album for six years *Black Tie White Noise* saw him reunite with *Let's Dance* producer Nile Rodgers.

Bowie's choice of producer for *Black Tie White Noise* was telling: Nile Rodgers, the man responsible for *Let's Dance*'s punchy dance grooves and gleaming pop sheen. Shuttling between Montreux, Los Angeles, and New York, Bowie and Rodgers pieced together the album over a period of several months, during which there were clashes over the direction of the record, with Bowie unimpressed by the Chic guitarist's attempts to revisit the direct, catchy approach of *Let's Dance*. Instead, the album became an interesting exercise in fusing contemporary dance-floor beats, slick 1970s soul, and free jazz. Several of the tracks featured trumpeter Lester Bowie, cofounder of the Art Ensemble of Chicago and a veteran of sessions with blues and soul artists such as Albert King and Solomon Burke and Afrobeat pioneer Fela Kuti. Elsewhere on the record, Mick Ronson was recruited to play guitar on a cover of Cream's "I Feel Free," which, together with "Looking for Lester," also featured the distinctive piano playing of pianist Mike Garson. Since parting company with Bowie after *Young Americans*, Garson had enjoyed a critically acclaimed solo career in jazz and renounced Scientology somewhere along the way.

One of the most powerful tracks on *Black Tie White Noise*, "Jump They Say," appeared to confront Terry Burns's suicide and became the unlikely choice for the first single off the album, which made the UK top spot in March 1993. In the States, *Black Tie White Noise* fared less well, largely because the label it appeared on, Savage, went bust not long after its release. In a curious twist, the company began legal proceedings against the singer to recoup some of its advance, but the case was thrown out of court.

Meanwhile, Bowie's status of an elder statesman of rock, respected by a new generation of young musicians, was underscored in an *NME* cover feature that paired Bowie with Brett Anderson of Britpop founding fathers, Suede, whose work was heavily and unashamedly shaded by the singer's 1970s canon. Bowie had already formed a mutual fan club with Morrissey, whose "I Know It's Gonna Happen Someday" was covered on *Black Tie White Noise*, and now offered a similar hand of friendship to Anderson, regarded by many as Morrissey's heir. "It was an amazing day for me, being such a fan," Anderson told the author. "What I remember most was how very charming, friendly, and funny Bowie was. He wasn't distant or difficult at all, which was how you might have imagined him to be. As an artist, what made him special was this brilliant ability he had to blend the mainstream and the avant-garde into one thing and still make it incredibly palatable. The image, the personality, it all needed to be present for it to work, but at the end of the day, it was the music."

Around the same time, *Interview* magazine dispatched novelist Hanif Kureishi to write a piece on the singer. Kureishi, raised in an Anglo-Pakistani household in Bromley, had won a prestigious Whitbread Book Award for his 1990 novel, *The Buddha of Suburbia*, which painted London's suburbs as landscapes that compelled their inhabitants

The Buddha of Suburbia

Original Soundtrack Album
Music written and performed by David Bowie
Produced by David Bowie and David Richards

to escape—a notion Bowie understood only too well. At the end of the meeting, the writer asked Bowie if he would contribute a song to the BBC's forthcoming TV dramatization of his book; Bowie's response was to offer instead to write the whole soundtrack. Working closely with Kureishi, the singer wrote around forty pieces of incidental music, as well as the title song. Then, just as he had with *Baal*, he reworked the music into a record of his own, employing Kizilçay and Garson to help him. The result was one of his most underrated works of the 1990s, an atmospheric and poignant record which crept out almost unnoticed on its release in November 1993—the same month Nirvana recorded its legendary *MTV Unplugged* performance, which unexpectedly paid homage to Bowie with a faithful cover of "The Man Who Sold the World."

Bowie's desire to return to his arty roots was signaled by his next move. At Bowie and Iman's wedding reception in 1992, the singer and Brian Eno had discussed working together again, and in early 1994, Bowie and his old Berlin Trilogy partner paid a visit to the Haus der Künstler, an artists' community within a psychiatric hospital near Vienna. The unit's approach to treating patients placed an emphasis on expression through painting and music, an idea that chimed with Bowie and Eno's interest in outsider art—and in themselves as outsider artists. Bowie assembled a band at Mountain Studios featuring Reeves Gabrels, Erdal Kizilçay, Mike Garson, and drummer Sterling Campbell. Under Eno's direction, a "game" commenced wherein the musicians were obliged to react to bizarre, *Oblique Strategies*-style commands and improvise atop other artists' records—after which the original source was erased—or simply compose together spontaneously. Other pieces were written by Bowie using a computer program that randomly jumbled sound files. "It was one of the most creative environments I've ever been in," Garson recalled to David Buckley.

Intrigued by the prevailing trend for piercings and tattoos, Bowie composed lyrical themes that explored the idea that the demise of religion had created a neo-paganist culture, with its own ritualistic behaviors and attitudes linking life, blood, art, and death. He'd also become interested in the legend surrounding the Minotaur of Crete, the fabulous creature of classical mythology that possessed a man's body and a bull's head and guarded the Labyrinth. These disparate elements were woven into a loose narrative

Bowie's soundtrack to *The Buddha of Suburbia*, which he wrote and recorded in six days and later cited as his favorite of his own albums.

Bowie took an increasing interest in computers in the 1990s, both as a songwriting aid and as a means to explore the new frontiers of the Internet.

Bowie's nineteenth album, *1. Outside*, reunited him with Brian Eno and was originally intended as the first in a second trilogy of collaborations. The cover image is a self-portrait entitled *The Dhead–Outside.head–Outside*.

for the record, previewed in *Q* magazine in December 1994 in the form of a short murder mystery story called "The Diary of Nathan Adler, or the Art-Ritual Murder of Baby Grace Blue." The plot involved a private detective recounting the cybernetic resurrection of a dead baby, with allusions to 1990s art and even to Bowie himself.

The album, which had the working title *Leon* and filled three CDs, was Bowie's most fully realized avant-garde work since the late 1970s. But, with Nirvana, Oasis, and Blur having made guitar records fashionable again, Bowie struggled to find a record label prepared to release it. In January 1995, he bowed to pressure and, with Alomar and Kevin Armstrong on guitar, created a more concise version of the album at New York's Hit Factory, adding more conventional—and superlative—new songs such as "No Control" and "We Prick You." Bowie also reworked the track "Hallo Spaceboy," a frantic industrial-pop hybrid evolved from a piece Reeves Gabrels had written called "Moondust," which fitted seamlessly into Bowie's career-spanning catalog of space-themed songs. In June 1995, a few weeks after Bowie exhibited his painting at a London gallery—including images of the Minotaur—he inked a deal with Virgin America and RCA/BMG in the UK. Three months later, the retitled *1. Outside* finally hit the racks, coinciding with the start of a year-long world tour which Bowie warned the public would *not* be a greatest hits package. Instead, the *1. Outside* tour aimed to revisit some of the neglected corners of his back catalog, including album tracks from the Berlin Trilogy, while also featuring a substantial chunk of *1. Outside*, whose haunting, hypnotic "The Heart's Filthy Lesson" was soon to become familiar to cinemagoers the world over as the end-credits music for David Fincher's noir-ish crime thriller *Seven*.

1. Outside was undoubtedly a masterpiece, and despite its experimental, anti-pop aesthetic, it fared well commercially, reaching No. 8 in the UK and No. 21 in the States. But the tour to promote it, with Nine Inch Nails as support on the US leg and Morrissey in the UK, was less enthusiastically received, with audiences confused by the esoteric setlist despite Bowie's attempts to make clear that it was far from tailored to the requirements of fair-weather fans. Bowie's performances, though, were among his most powerful ever, bolstered by a touring band that featured an intriguing mix of familiar faces—Reeves Gabrels, Carlos Alomar, Mike Garson, and backing singer George Simms—and young blood—bassist Gail Ann Dorsey, drummer Zachary Alford, and keyboardist/musical director Peter Schwartz.

During a month-long summer break in August 1996, Bowie took the group into Philip Glass's New York studio to work on *1. Outside*'s follow-up, *Earthling*, which, with the singer's antennae ever attuned to the new, co-opted pounding techno and drum 'n' bass rhythms for several tracks, reflecting his and Gabrels's fondness for dance acts such as Prodigy and Underworld. A key collaborator on the project was engineer Mark Plati, who'd worked as part of 1980s dance pioneer Arthur Baker's production team,

A ticket for one of Bowie's fall 1995 European shows with Morrissey, who ended up withdrawing from the tour after nine dates.

Bowie onstage with Trent Reznor of Nine Inch Nails, with whom he co-headlined a run of North American shows in support of *I. Outside*, at the Meadowlands Arena in East Rutherford, New Jersey, September 28, 1995.

The cover art to *Earthling*, which shows Bowie in a Union Jack frockcoat designed by Alexander McQueen.

leading to sessions with Quincy Jones, Janet Jackson, and Prince. Alford's drum patterns became the focus of particular attention, and programmed loops and live drums exquisitely meshed to create *Earthling*'s complex beats. The following month, the album's stirring calling card "Little Wonder" was incorporated into the band's set and plans were hatched to launch the album—whose cover pictured Bowie with rakish goatee and the distressed Union flag frockcoat he'd worn on the summer festival dates—at a special concert at Madison Square Garden in January 1997 to celebrate his fiftieth birthday.

The Madison Square Garden show, staged on January 9, the day after Bowie reached his half century, was an opportunity for his biggest fans in contemporary music to pay their respects. Pixies' Frank Black joined the singer for "Scary Monsters" and "Fashion," Foo Fighters pitched in for "Hallo Spaceboy," the Cure's Robert Smith had a duet with Bowie on "Quicksand," Sonic Youth pulverized *Earthling*'s "I'm Afraid of Americans," a grinning Lou Reed growled his way through a medley of Velvet Underground numbers, and Smashing Pumpkins' Billy Corgan took the stage for "All the Young Dudes" and "The Jean Genie." Quizzed where he saw his career going from here, Bowie replied, "I have no idea . . . but I promise I won't bore you."

The *Earthling* tour ran from June to November 1997, and the eclectic setlist met with the same mixed reaction as the *Outside* dates had. In the UK, the album—which twenty years on still sounds contemporary with its alluring collision of atmospheric pop, dog-fighting guitars, industrial grind, and fuzzy electronica—reached No. 6, though in the States it barely scraped the Top 40. But with Bowie's ability to confound also came an impulse to surprise. At the Phoenix Festival at Stratford-upon-Avon in July, Bowie preceded his Sunday night headlining slot with a storming secret "guerrilla gig" the previous day in the dance tent, performing a drum 'n' bass set under the guise of the Tao Jones Index.

Bowie prepares to blow out the candles on his fiftieth birthday cake at Madison Square Garden, New York, January 9, 1997.

The pun on the Dow Jones index was timely: in 1997, Bowie's outsider thinking had expanded to his fiscal dealings. Using an innovation dreamed up by finance guru David Pullman, that September Bowie floated his back catalog on the stock exchange via a concept dubbed Bowie Bonds, whereby investors could secure a share of the singer's future royalties for a ten-year term. As sales of Bowie's old records were topping a million copies a year, the idea was an attractive one.

The scheme instantly netted Bowie around $55 million, which, ingeniously, he used to buy out Tony Defries's stake in the recordings he'd made up until 1982. The rest of the money he reinvested in the stock market to buy back the bonds when they expired. Such was the brilliance of the plan that the "Celebrity Bond" soon became a popular way for artists to exploit the fruits of their past labors. Pullman later commented that "David was an intuitive guy. He picked up on [the concept] instantaneously."

As the millennium approached, Bowie's interest in exploring intriguing new avenues outside music continued to develop. An early adopter of the Internet, Bowie had engaged in webchats with fans since the *1. Outside* era, and in 1998 he unveiled his own websites, davidbowie.com and bowieart.com. Soon after, these were joined by an Internet provider, BowieNet. The singer's enthusiasm for state-of-the-art technology became the catalyst for his next album, *Hours*, which developed from the soundtrack he'd been asked to write for a video game, *Omikron: The Nomad Soul*, designed by the company behind *Tomb Raider*. The game featured Bowie as a character named Boz, leader of the Awakened, though he also appeared as an avatar of himself performing at venues around Omikron City with Reeves Gabrels and Gail Ann Dorsey.

Most of the recording for the album took place in Bermuda, with Bowie and Gabrels helming a studio group including Mark Plati (playing bass and synths as well as programming) and drummers Sterling Campbell and Mike Levesque. Bowie's aim was to combine contemporary digital studio techniques with old-fashioned chord progressions and melodies, an approach that would lend tracks such as "Thursday's Child," "If I'm Dreaming My Life," and "Seven," an enchanting, self-questioning, nostalgic atmosphere, chiming with album's lyrical preoccupations with past relationships, mortality, childhood memories, and the nature of existence. There were solid rockers too, including the *Idiot*-like "The Pretty Things Are Going to Hell," a song acknowledging the possible fate of

The reflective *Hours*, released in 1999, saw Bowie look backward for the first time in his career.

(opposite)
Bowie onstage at the Astoria, London, during the short tour in support of *Hours*, December 2, 1999.

(opposite)
Bowie onstage at the Glastonbury Festival, June 25, 2000—his first time back since 1971.

Bowie and his beautiful generation. Released in September 1999, with artwork that showed a contemporary, long-haired Bowie cradling his moribund, short-haired 1990s self, *Hours* was a powerful restatement of his gifts as a conventional songwriter, though following the downward path of his 1990s sales graph, it failed to make the Billboard Top 40 in the United States, the first Bowie album to suffer this fate since *Ziggy Stardust*.

But even if the investors in his Bowie Bonds were unduly fretting (though when the bonds expired in 2007, the shareholders' original investment was paid back in full), the first weeks of the twenty-first century found Bowie on a creative and emotional high—the latter not least because in February 2000 it was announced that he and Iman were expecting a child. With parenthood looming yet again, Bowie attempted to quit smoking, leading to a series of minor health issues. For the first time in his career, a Bowie concert—one of three that June at New York's Roseland Ballroom—was canceled due to a bout of laryngitis. The dates, which saw Earl Slick rejoining the band, replacing Reeves Gabrels after his and Bowie's relationship had cooled, were warmups for a headlining slot at the Glastonbury Festival, the first time Bowie had played at Pilton Farm since his 5:00 a.m. performance in 1971.

It was perhaps this completion of a circle, and the dawning of a new century, that influenced the singer's decision to record an album of remakes of his "lost" late-60s classics, including "The London Boys," "Can't Help Thinking About Me," "You've Got a Habit of Leaving," and "Let Me Sleep Beside You." The sessions, which took place in New York just a month before his and Iman's daughter, Alexandria, was born, were penciled in for release the following year under the title *Toy*, after a new song written for the project. But it in a move that Bowie found immensely dispiriting, EMI/Virgin refused to release

A ticket and program for the 2000 Glastonbury Festival, headlined by Bowie, Travis, and the Chemical Brothers.

Bowie gives a solemn reading of Paul Simon's "America" to open the *Concert for New York City* at Madison Square Garden, October 20, 2001.

the album, insisting he should deliver a record of fresh material first. The issue was never resolved and precipitated the artist's ill-tempered split with the company in 2001. (The song "Toy" later became the Internet-only track "Your Turn to Drive," while the rest of the album would also eventually trickle out in various forms.)

Ironically, while *Toy* hung in limbo, Bowie was already at work on a record of all-new material, reuniting him with producer Tony Visconti, whose last major project with the singer had been *Scary Monsters*. Visconti had worked with Bowie on the string arrangements for *Toy*, as well as other recordings, but their renewed friendship didn't become public knowledge until the producer joined Bowie on bass for an appearance at the charity House Benefit Concert at Carnegie Hall. The majority of what would become *Heathen* was laid down that summer at Allaire Studios, a facility hidden away in the Catskill Mountains 150 miles north of New York. Bowie found the remote location, two thousand feet above sea level and overlooking a reservoir teaming with wildlife, inspirational, explaining that when he first went there, "It was almost like my feet were lifted off the ground."

The beautiful, barren, tranquil landscape reflected his meditative state of mind: his mother, Peggy, had died in April, aged eighty-eight, at a nursing home in Saint Albans, while the following month Freddie Burretti, who designed some of Bowie's most iconic 1970s costumes, passed away in Paris. While *Hours* had contemplated mortality, the lyrics that Bowie rose at 6:00 a.m. each day to write went further, seemingly describing

The cover art to the last two albums Bowie released before disappearing from public view: the contemplative *Heathen* and the more band-oriented *Reality.*

the moment of death on the mournful title track and questioning his faith in a higher being on the plaintive, gentle "A Better Future." He also ventured into the stars once again with a cover of the Legendary Stardust Cowboy's "I Took a Trip on a Gemini Spaceship," a rare moment of light humor. The otherwise sad, contemplative feel of the record took on a new purpose when, while Bowie and Visconti were mixing the record in New York, the twin towers of the World Trade Center came under attack. Since he'd sold his property in Lausanne in 1998, Bowie had become an inveterate New Yorker, loving the family-centered life he led at his Broadway condominium—so it was perhaps only natural that he should join in the Concert for New York City, staged on October 20, to remember those killed in the 9/11 attacks.

When *Heathen* was released in June 2002, many reviewers assumed it was a response to the tragic events in New York the previous September, but Bowie and Visconti took pains to explain that its interrogations of religion and what the future might bring dated to before the attacks. The sleeve, showing Bowie with deathly, fishlike eyes, was later revealed to be a coded reference to Christianity, the fish being the secret symbol of early Christians, as well as to *Un Chien Andalou*'s gruesome eyeball surgery. The sophisticated layering of the music and imagery was, Bowie stressed, essential for a record that by its very nature commanded high expectations. "Obviously a lot of crafting went into the new material," he told *MOJO*'s Paul Du Noyer. "I was determined that Tony and I shouldn't rest on previous reputations. Such a lot of the albums we did together are held up in fairly high esteem and we didn't want to tarnish that."

Heathen's release coincided with Bowie's curation of the annual Meltdown festival on London's South Bank, with a handpicked bill of established acts featuring the Divine Comedy, Coldplay, Suede, Mercury Rev, and Supergrass, together with such cult delights as the Legendary Stardust Cowboy and Daniel Johnston, and the London Sinfonietta performing Philip Glass's orchestral versions of *Low* and

"Heroes". The final night of Meltdown starred Bowie himself, launching the *Heathen* tour with a group featuring Earl Slick, Dublin-born guitarist Gerry Leonard, Mark Plati, Gail Ann Dorsey, Mike Garson, Sterling Campbell, and backing vocalist and keyboard player Catherine Russell. With a who's who of celebrity Bowie fans in attendance, from Bono and Brian Eno to Tracey Emin and Kylie Minogue, Bowie gave a masterful performance and dedicated the new album's poignant "5:15 The Angels Have Gone" to the Who's John Entwistle, who had died the previous day.

Heathen had been released by Columbia in conjunction with Bowie's own ISO label, and a healthy marketing budget helped push it to No. 14 in the States and No. 3 in the UK. The "comfortable" arrangement the singer enjoyed with the company, which agreed to distribute his material when it was ready, had the unexpected consequence of a new Bowie album dropping just fifteen months later. Recorded in New York in the first half of 2003, *Reality* featured members of Bowie's *Heathen* tour band in spirited rock mode, with Gerry Leonard's heavily treated guitar textures the defining component of a record whose edgy sonic signature owed much to *Scary Monsters*. Visconti's bass playing, which survived on several tracks from the initial demos he and Bowie had recorded, also added vital character, while Mike Garson's distinctive piano playing was clearly evident

The Bowie band warms up for *A Reality Tour* at the Chance nightclub, in Poughkeepsie, New York, August 19, 2003. From left: Earl Slick, Mike Garson, Bowie, Sterling Campbell, Gail Ann Dorsey, and Gerry Leonard (not shown: Mark Plati and Catherine Russell).

on the jazzy, Sinatra-esque lament of "Bring Me the Disco King" and the gorgeously lachrymose deep soul of "The Loneliest Guy."

Thematically, *Reality* was just about that: how the events in the outside world are distorted through the prism of the media to create a reality that is entirely artificial and also how experience colors the way any individual sees the world. The point of view of the album changes with the characters in each song, from the unpleasant protagonist of "Fall Dog Bombs the Moon" and disabused romantic of "She'll Drive the Big Car" to the regretful narrators of "Bring Me the Disco King" and "The Loneliest Guy."

The *A Reality* tour—its name gamely suggesting the reality it presented was merely one of many—kicked off in Copenhagen on October 7, and with around 130 dates, it was set to be one of Bowie's longest ever. The group rehearsed a total of fifty songs, from which around twenty-five were performed each night, juggling the singer's millennial output with old favorites. In December 2003, however, there were early warning signs that Bowie, who had admitted the previous year that "touring gets harder at my age," was feeling the strain of the punishing schedule. Five gigs at the start of the North American leg of the tour were canceled due to a bout of influenza and rescheduled for the following year. When the tour resumed, all seemed well until a date in Oslo on June 18, 2004, when Bowie was hit in the eye with a lollipop thrown from the crowd. Bowie quipped, "Lucky you hit the bad one," but it proved to be a portentous omen.

In Prague five days later, the singer left the stage after nine songs with excruciating chest pains. He returned to sing two more songs then brought the show to a halt. Then, after performing a full set at the Hurricane Festival at Scheeßel in Germany on June 25, Bowie was rushed to hospital and underwent heart surgery the following day. The rest of the tour was canceled, effectively putting Bowie's career on ice for the next ten years. Although he subsequently appeared in public as a guest of other artists such as Arcade Fire and David Gilmour and made cameo appearances in films and on TV, Bowie would never tour again. There would be no new album, either, until he sensationally re-emerged in 2013—with what would be his penultimate record.

January 8, 2013, was a relatively slow news day, dominated by a report that a US drone attack had killed eight people in Pakistan. Music websites noted that Elvis Presley would have turned seventy-eight had he not died in 1977 and also that it was David Bowie's sixty-sixth birthday. But since Bowie had shunned the public's gaze since introducing a show by British comedian Ricky Gervais at Madison Square Garden in May 2007, few saw much significance in the anniversary. Then news broke that the singer had posted a brand-new song on his website, together with a video. The rush to hear the track with which Bowie had broken his seven-year silence—also dropped into

Bowie, backed by guitarist Earl Slick and keyboard wizard Mike Garson, at the 112th and final show on the *Reality* tour at the Hurricane Festival in Scheessel, Germany, June 26, 2004.

A ticket for the second of two *Reality* shows at Wembley Arena, London, November 26, 2003.

iTunes without any warning for fans to purchase—was accelerated by news that it was a taster for an album. The song, titled "Where Are We Now?," was a wistful, stunningly beautiful piece in which Bowie appeared to be recalling his late 1970s sojourn in Berlin, with references to the Dschungel nightclub, Potsdamer Platz railway station, and the KaDeWe department store. Its elegiac air was lent added poignancy by the video, directed by New Yorker Tony Oursler, which showed Bowie and a female companion as puppets with distorted faces, and Bowie as himself wearing a T-shirt bearing the legend *Song of Norway*—the film musical that in 1969 Hermione Farthingale traveled overseas to work on, breaking his heart when she fell in love with an actor on the set. Bowie declined to do any promotion for the release, the task falling to Tony Visconti, who produced the material. "When 'Where Are We Now?' came out, I knew that people were almost going to have a heart attack," Visconti told writer Keith Cameron. "*That* was exciting. I don't think we'll reproduce that feeling again."

Bowie had started working on what would become *The Next Day* in 2011, after emailing members of his *A Reality* tour band asking whether they were available for recording sessions in New York. Bowie was determined to keep the project secret so the album could take shape without any pressure from his record label or the media. "The first thing he did is hand out NDAs [Non-Disclosure Agreements] to people," Zachary Alford said in the BBC documentary *The Last Five Years*. "That had never happened before." The first sessions for the album took place at Human World Wide studios with Sterling Campbell on drums, Visconti on bass, Gerry Leonard on guitar, and Bowie on keyboards. After just twenty-four hours, concerns that news of Bowie's presence in the studio had leaked out meant the operation transferred to the Magic Shop in SoHo,

where work continued for a week. Then, according to Visconti, "we heard nothing for four months." Recording eventually resumed in summer 2012 with contributions from other musicians, including Alford, Gail Ann Dorsey, Earl Slick, David Torn, and saxophonist Steve Elson. Over the next few months, Bowie and Visconti did further work on the tapes, the singer taking his time "so he could finish every song to perfection," said Visconti.

The album was released in March 2013, preceded by another single, "The Stars (Are Out Tonight)," a wry comment on celebrity culture set against an undulating, enchanting art-rock backing strongly redolent of Bowie's late-'70s work. The idea that *The Next Day* might share a musical commonality with the Berlin Trilogy and *Scary Monsters* was further insinuated by its cover, created by Jonathan Barnbrook, which took the Masayoshi Sukita portrait of Bowie used on the cover of *"Heroes"* and defaced it with a white square bearing the album's title. This notion of echoing the past while firmly

Bowie makes what had become by now an increasingly rare public appearance alongside his son, director Duncan Jones, at the Tribeca Film Festival, April 30, 2009.

A promotional poster for the record-breaking *David Bowie Is* exhibition at the Victoria and Albert Museum, London.

existing in the present was borne out by tracks such as "Valentine's Day," a mellifluous rocker seemingly describing a high-school shooting, and the unsettling bass and synthesizer pulse of "Love Is Lost," which may or may not allude to Bowie's first brush with fame in 1969. "I'd Rather Be High" is written from the perspective of a conscientious objector serving as a soldier in the North African desert in World War II, a story resonating powerfully with contemporary events in the Middle East. Starved of new Bowie product for almost a decade, reviewers were overwhelmingly ecstatic at *The Next Day*'s superlative lyrical quality and reassuring sonic familiarity, and with the help of positive notices, the record immediately claimed the No. 1 spot in the UK and reached No. 2 in the States.

Yet Bowie himself remained elusive, a fleeting shadowy figure newly shrouded in mystique as a sixty-something Howard Hughes of rock. There would, the world was informed through Visconti, be no live dates to promote the album, though the producer was subsequently asked by Bowie's management to soften his statement intimating the singer would never play live again. The fact of the matter was that Bowie was itching to get on with recording a follow-up to *The Next Day* but realized that it would be better to wait until he had more fully developed song ideas. Visconti didn't have to wait long until he got the call: in June 2014, Bowie contacted the producer and arranged a two-day session to "fool around with a few concepts." When they finished, there were five new songs sketched out. To Visconti's surprise, Bowie also brought in a batch of demos that he'd made at home, something he'd never done before. One of these was "'Tis a Pity She Was a Whore," destined for a release that November as part of a separate project that Bowie and Visconti had become involved with.

For several years, Bowie had been fascinated with the work of Maria Schneider, a classically trained composer who led her own big band jazz orchestra based in Greenwich Village. Schneider

Bowie's last two studio albums: the surprise return *The Next Day* from 2013, and the majestic *Blackstar* (page 216), released two days before his death in 2016.

was an early adopter of crowdfunding, using the method to fund her Grammy-winning 2004 album *Concert in the Garden*, as big bands were particularly expensive to record. Bowie called Schneider and asked her to collaborate with him on "'Tis a Pity She Was a Whore" and another new song, "Sue (Or in a Season of Crime)." "Sue" ended up as a mind-blowing, avant-garde, big-band-jazz mash-up that was included, as the opening track, on *Nothing Has Changed*, a three-CD compilation surveying Bowie's whole career from 1964's "Liza Jane" to *The Next Day*—the first time such an ambitious retrospective had been attempted. The soulful saxophone solo on the track had been played by the jazz orchestra's Donny McCaslin, whose own progressive jazz combo Schneider urged Bowie to check out. Bowie snuck virtually unnoticed into one of their gigs at the 55 Bar on Christopher Street in the autumn of 2014 and told them, with characteristic charm, that he'd be honored if they would guest on his next album. "He did his research on us," bassist Tim Lefebvre told writer Danny Eccleston, "Watched YouTubes of us. He'd brought [drummer] Mark Guiliana's *Beat Music*, which I'm also on. Usually it's the other way around—you research the guy who hired you."

In December 2014, Bowie contacted Visconti to say he'd written several more songs, and in January they booked into the Magic Shop to begin crafting the material with McCaslin's group, a process that continued in short bursts for the next three months. "Their approach to the music was so refreshing, I looked forward every day to the studio. Nothing was done recalling the past. There was one part where we were overdubbing just for the guitar tone. I had to inform [guitarist] Ben Monder how Mick Ronson would have done it and he looked at me blankly. It was interesting teaching a jazz guy how to play rock!"

The music essayed on the album was unlike anything Bowie had created before—cosmic free jazz of a deeply expressive kind, incorporating elements of hip hop and electronica, given a singular purpose by lyrics that came from a dark, strange, ostensibly unfathomable place. On "Blackstar," the title track of the album (represented as ★), Bowie incanted an Eastern-flavored melody over a two-step beat, murmuring about "the day of execution" before the song transforms into a more hymnal-sounding Bowie epic, as he declares, "Somebody took his place and bravely cried: I'm a blackstar!" The sessions also yielded remakes of "Sue" and "'Tis a Pity She Was a Whore," which, shorn of their big-band arrangements, enabled McCaslin's players to scale even grander heights of sonic discombobulation. The mournful groove of the album-closing "I Can't Give Everything Away" echoed the harmonica riff of *Low*'s "A New Career in a New Town," a rare nod to Bowie's past that added to *Blackstar*'s ominous, disquieting atmosphere. But of the album's seven tracks, it was the plaintive "Lazarus" that packed the greatest emotional punch, beginning with the perturbing couplet, "Look up here, I'm in heaven / I've got scars that can't be seen."

What fans didn't know when "Lazarus" was made available as a download in the week prior to Christmas 2015 was that Bowie was sending the world a message—he was dying. On January 7, 2016, a video for the single, shot by Swedish director Johan Renck, was released, showing Bowie lying in a hospital bed, blindfolded with a bandage that had a button sewn atop each eye. For the last eighteen months, Bowie had been fighting liver cancer, and in the week the video was filmed, he'd been told he had only days to live. Renck remembers Bowie singing along with the words to the song as he was filmed, giving one last passionate performance for the public. Renck had also made an eleven-minute film to accompany "Blackstar," loaded with the haunting, heart-wrenching image of the body of a dead astronaut—Major Tom— whose bones are taken away to become relics. *Blackstar* was released on the singer's sixty-ninth birthday—January 8—and on January 10, news broke to a shocked and unsuspecting world that Bowie had died at home in his New York apartment.

Tributes flowed in to a man who, over four decades, had been instrumental in transforming rock music into an extraordinary art form, approaching each of his twenty-six studio albums as blank canvases on which to paint something vital, new, and original, while also sculpting himself into myriad fascinating characters, from Ziggy Stardust and Aladdin Sane to Halloween Jack, the Thin White Duke, and the bleach-blond matinee idol of *Let's Dance*. He had achieved something truly great—he'd changed the language of sound. His parallel career as an actor meant that, in Bowie's hands, music was always something inherently theatrical and audio-visual, forever designed to challenge audiences rather than simply entertain them. Visconti's response to Bowie's death was, perhaps unsurprisingly, deeply personal, moving, and insightful. "He always did what he wanted to do," the producer wrote. "And he wanted to do it his way and the best way. His death was no different from his life—a work of art. . . . He was an extraordinary man, full of love and life. He will always be with us. For now, it's appropriate to cry."

But Bowie's gifts to the world of the arts didn't end with *Blackstar*. On December 7, 2015, just a month before he passed away, Bowie had attended the opening night at the New York Theatre Workshop production of *Lazarus*, a play he'd devised with the Belgian theater director Ivo van Hove. The

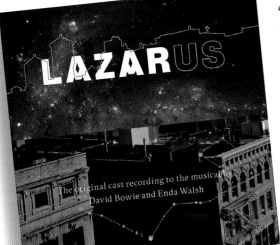

The original cast recording to the musical by David Bowie and Enda Walsh

The original cast recording of *Lazarus*, Bowie's stage collaboration with Enda Walsh and Ivo van Hove.

From left: Jason Lindner, Mark Guiliana, Donny McCaslin, and Tim Lefebvre—co-winners, with Bowie, of the Grammy Award for "Best Alternative Music Album" for *Blackstar*.

work, written by Bowie and Irish playwright Enda Walsh, was a loose sequel to *The Man Who Fell to Earth* and used fifteen songs from Bowie's back catalog together with three new compositions. While *Rolling Stone* called it "theatre at its finest," Bowie biographer Paul Trynka concluded that "at its best, it's staggering beautiful" and found it "frequently profound." One trusts that before his death, Bowie read these critical bouquets for his play, which was revived to similar acclaim in London in the winter of 2016/17.

In 2002, he'd remarked of his career, "I had really wanted to write musicals more than anything else." And so, in his final days, arguably the greatest rock star that ever lived happily and masterfully fulfilled his teenage dream.

Flowers pile up in front of a memorial to Bowie in Brixton, London, on the day after his death in January 2016.

Sources

BOOKS

Bowie, Angela, with Patrick Carr. *Backstage Passes: Life on the Wild Side With David Bowie*, Cooper Square, 2000.

Buckley, David. *Strange Fascination: David Bowie: The Definitive Story*, Virgin, 2005.

Finnigan, Mary. *Psychedelic Suburbia: David Bowie and the Beckenham Arts Lab*, Jorvik Press, 2016.

Gillman, Peter & Leni. *Alias David Bowie*, Henry Holt & Co, 1987.

Goddard, Simon. *Ziggyology: A Brief History of Ziggy Stardust*, Ebury Press, 2015.

Pegg, Nicholas. *The Complete David Bowie*, Titan, 2016.

Pitt, Kenneth. *Bowie: The Pitt Report*, Music Sales, 1985.

Trynka, Paul. *Starman: David Bowie: The Definitive Biography*, Sphere, 2012.

Visconti, Tony. *The Autobiography: Bowie, Bolan and the Brooklyn Boy*, Harper, 2007.

Woodmansey, Woody. *Spider From Mars: My Life With David Bowie*, Sidgwick & Jackson, 2016.

BOOK-A-ZINES

MOJO: Bowie Special Limited Edition, EMAP, 2003.

MOJO Classic: Bowie 60 Years Of…, EMAP, 2007.

INTERVIEWS

Coxhill, Gordon. "Don't Dig Too Deep, Pleads David Bowie," *New Musical Express*, November 1969.

Watts, Michael. "Oh You Pretty Thing," *Melody Maker*, January 1972.

Shaar Murray, Charles. "David at the Dorchester," *New Musical Express*, July 1972.

————. "Goodbye Ziggy and a Big Hello to Aladdin Sane," *New Musical Express*, 1973.

Hilburn, Robert. "Bowie Finds His Voice," *Melody Maker*, September 1974.

————. "Now I'm a Businessman," *Melody Maker*, February 1976.

Jones, Allan. "Goodbye to Ziggy and All That," *Melody Maker*, October 1977.

Tobler, John. "12 Minutes with David Bowie," *ZigZag*, January 1978.

Watts, Michael. "Confession of an Elitist," *Melody Maker*, February 1978.

MacKinnon, Angus. "The Future Isn't What It Used To Be," *New Musical Express*, September 1980.

Thomas, David. "The Interview," *The Face*, May 1983.

Shaar Murray, Charles. "Sermon from the Savoy," *New Musical Express*, September 1984.

Deevoy, Adrian. "Boys Keep Swinging," *Q*, June 1989.

Sutherland, Steve. "One Day, Son, All This Could Be Yours. . . ," *New Musical Express*, March 1993.

Sinclair, David. "Station to Station," *Rolling Stone*, June 1993.

Cavanagh, David. "ChangesFiftyBowie," *Q*, February 1997.

Quantick, David. "Now Where Did I Put Those Tunes?" *Q*, October 1999.

Du Noyer, Paul. "Contact," *MOJO*, July 2002.

————. "Do You Remember Your First Time?" November 2003.

WEBSITES

BowieNet, www.davidbowie.com

Teenage Wildlife, www.teenagewildlife.com

Pushing Ahead of the Dame, www.bowiesongs.wordpress.com

Ziggy Stardust Companion, www.5years.com

TV DOCUMENTARIES

Five Years, BBC 4, directed by Francis Whately, 2013.

The Last Five Years, BBC 2, directed by Francis Whately, 2016.

Image Credits

a=all, b=bottom, i=inset, l=left, r=right, t=top

Alamy Stock Photos: p2, Pictorial Press Ltd; p12, Pictorial Press Ltd; p16, Pictorial Press Ltd; p18, R. Ward/ Pictorial Press Ltd; p24t, Pictorial Press Ltd; p24b, Kevin Cann/Pictorial Press Ltd; p26t, Pictorial Press Ltd; p27, Pictorial Press Ltd; p32, Tracksimages.com; p33, Pictorial Press Ltd; p45, Pictorial Press Ltd; p50, Trinity Mirror/Mirrorpix; p52, Trinity Mirror/Mirrorpix; p55, Pictorial Press Ltd; p59, Trinity Mirror/Mirrorpix; p60, Pictorial Press Ltd; p78t, Pictorial Press Ltd; p94b, ZUMA Press, Inc.; p96, Pictorial Press Ltd; p97, Trinity Mirror/Mirrorpix; p99, Pictorial Press Ltd; p111, Everett Collection; p114, Harold Smith; p128, Trinity Mirror/Mirrorpix; p133, Collection Christophel; p137, dpa picture alliance; p147, Keystone/ZUMA Press, Inc.; p184, Antiques & Collectables; p207b, Mark Kerrison. **Andrew Smyth Collection:** p63blr; p77b; p78b; p79; p100a; p117a; p121a; p142; p144a; p151a; p154blr; p155blr; p157b; p163; p177t; p177bl; p181t; p193b; p202t; p207b; p212b. **Associated Press:** p23, Dezo Hoffmann; p38, Ray Stevenson; p40t, REX Features; p166, Marty Lederhandler. **Bridgeman Images:** p161, Private Collection/Christie's Images; p172b, DILTZ; p173t; p173b, Collection CSFF; p191, DILTZ. **Getty Images:** Endpapers, Steve Wood/Express/Hulton; p1, Terry O'Neill; p5, Gijsbert Hanekroot/Redferns; p6, Ebet Roberts/Redferns; p9, Chris Lopez/Sony Music Archive; pp10–11, Gijsbert Hanekroot/Redferns; p13, Cyrus Andrews/Michael Ochs Archives; p17, Fiona Adams/ Redferns; p19, Hulton-Deutsch Collection/CORBIS via Getty Images; p22, *Evening Standard*; p26b, Don Paulsen/Michael Ochs Archives; p30, Photoshot/Hulton Archive; p34, Mark and Colleen Hayward; p35, Debi Doss/Hulton Archive; p36b, RB/Redferns; p39t, RB/Redferns; p42, Michael Ochs Archives; p51, Earl Leaf/ Michael Ochs Archives; p57, Lynn Goldsmith/CORBIS; p61, M. Stroud/*Daily Express*; p62, Michael Ochs Archives; p64, Michael Putland; p65, John Lynn Kirk/Redferns; p67, Michael Ochs Archives; p68, Michael Ochs Archives; p71, Michael Putland; p72, Michael Ochs Archives; p74, Michael Putland; p76, Gus Stewart/Redferns; p81, John Lynn Kirk/Redferns; p83t, Michael Ochs Archives; p84, Michael Ochs Archives; p86, Richard Creamer/Michael Ochs Archives; pp88 and 89, Gijsbert Hanekroot/Redferns; p91t, Debi Doss/Redferns; p92t, Mark and Colleen Hayward; p92b, Bettmann; p93, Debi Doss/Redferns; p95b, Jack Kay/*Daily Express*; p98, Michael Ochs Archives; p103, Michael Ochs Archives; p104, Terry O'Neill/Iconic Images; p109, Bettmann; p116t, British Lion Film Corporation/Sunset Boulevard/CORBIS; p118, Mark Sullivan/Hulton Archive; p119, Michael Ochs Archives; p120, Michael Ochs Archives; p122, Michael Ochs Archives; pp124–125, Michael Marks/Donaldson Collection; p130, Ian Dickson/Redferns; p134, Roberta Bayley/Redferns; p139, RDA; p140, Richard McCaffrey/Michael Ochs Archives; p143, Michael Ochs Archives; p150, Jacques Dejean/ Sygma; p152, Peter Still/Redferns; p153, Larry Hulst/Michael Ochs Archives; p156, Robin Platzer/The LIFE Images Collection; p159, Gary Gershoff; p160, Koh Hasebe/Shinko Music; p170t, Ebet Roberts/Redferns; p178,AFP; p179, Fotos International; p180, LGI Stock/CORBIS; p182, Dave Hogan; p187, KMazur/WireImage; p188t, Dave Hogan; p188bl, RB/Redferns; p190, Larry Busacca/Wireimage; p192, Rob Verhorst/Redferns; p195b, Rob Verhorst/Redferns; p197, Rose Hartman/WireImage; p201t, Time & LIFE Pictures; p202b, KMazur/WireImage; p203b, KMazur/WireImage; p205, Nicky J. Sims/Redferns; p206, Andy Willsher/Redferns; p208, Scott Gries/ImageDirect; p210, KMazur/WireImage; p212t, Malzkorn/ullstein bild; p213, Michael Loccisano/Getty Images for Tribeca Film Festival; p217t, Jason LaVeris/FilmMagic. **REX/Shutterstock:** p20; p36t, Ray Stevenson; p37, Ray Stevenson; p39b, Ray Stevenson; p44, Ray Stevenson; pp58–59, ITV; p90t, R. Bamber; p101, Les Lambert; p116b, StudioCanal; p127, Kypros; p135, MediaPunch; p146, ITV; p162, Richard Young; p165b, Robert Rosen; p168, Ron Galella/WireImage; p174, Andre Csillag. **Voyageur Press Collection:** p15; p21; p25; pp28–29a; p31; p40b; p41; p46; p47a; p49; p53; p63t; p73, p75; p77t; p82b; p83b; p85; p90b; p91b; p94t; p95t; p100b; p102; p107; p112; p113; p115; p122a; p127a; p131; p136; p141; p145; p148a; p150i; p154t; p155t; p164; p165t; p170b; p171a; p172t; p176; p177br; p181b; p183; p188br; p189a; p191i; p193t; p195t; p196; p198a; p200; p201b; p203t; p204; p209b; p214a; p216a.

Index

About the Author

PAT GILBERT has been writing about music and film for over twenty-five years. He is a former editor of *MOJO*, the world's biggest-selling music magazine, and these days edits its offshoot, *MOJO '60s*. Pat is also the author of *Passion Is A Fashion*, the definitive biography of The Clash, and has provided sleeve notes for the group's official releases since the late '90s. In 2002, he had the honor of stepping aside from his *MOJO* role for a month to enable David Bowie to guest-edit the magazine. Pat lives in London, not far from Bowie's old family home in Bromley.